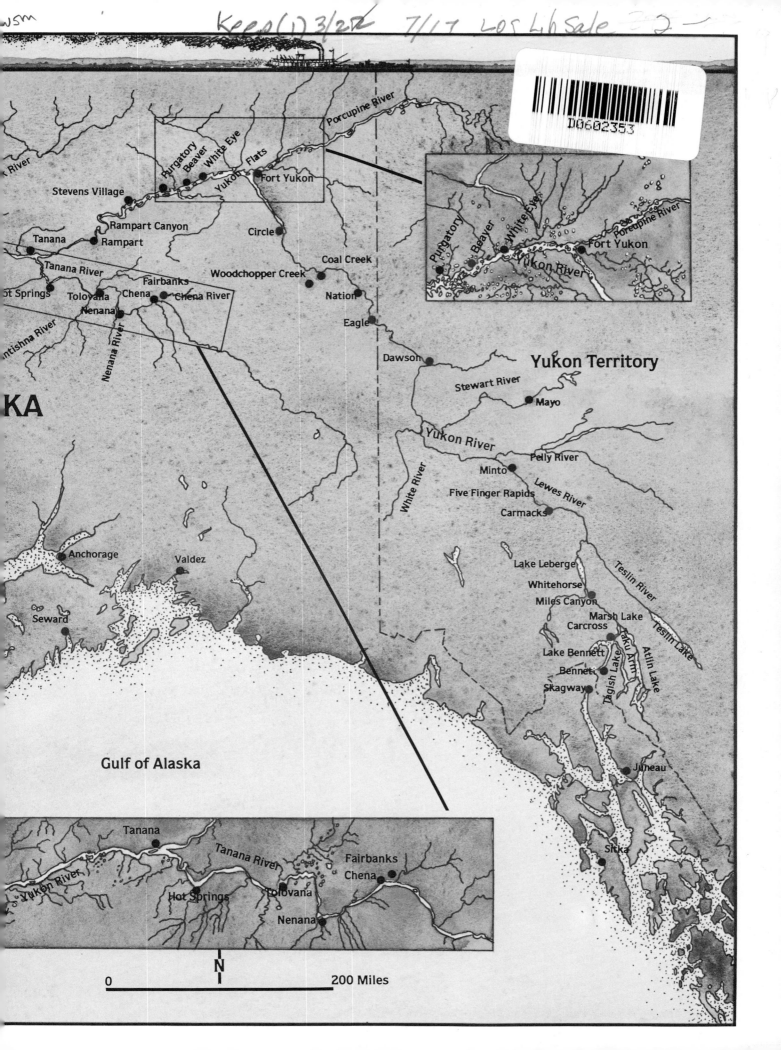

Porcupine River

Purgatory
Beaver
White Eye
Yukon Flats
Fort Yukon

Stevens Village

Rampart Canyon

Tanana
Rampart

Circle

Tanana River

Coal Creek

Woodchopper Creek

Hot Springs
Tolovana
Chena
Fairbanks
Chena River

Nation

Nenana

Nenana River

Eagle

ntishna River

KA

Dawson

Yukon Territory

Stewart River

Mayo

Yukon River

Pelly River

Minto

Five Finger Rapids
Lewes River

Carmacks

White River

Lake Leberge

Teslin River

Whitehorse

Miles Canyon

Anchorage

Valdez

Marsh Lake
Carcross

Teslin Lake

Lake Bennett

Taku Arm

Atlin Lake

Bennett

Tagish Lake

Seward

Skagway

Purgatory
Beaver
White Eye
Fort Yukon
Porcupine River
Yukon River

Gulf of Alaska

Juneau

Sitka

Tanana

Tanana River

Fairbanks
Chena

Yukon River

Hot Springs
Tolovana

Nenana

N

0   200 Miles

LIFELINE TO THE YUKON

A HISTORY OF YUKON RIVER NAVIGATION

LIFELINE TO THE YUKON

A HISTORY OF YUKON RIVER NAVIGATION

BY

BARRY C. ANDERSON

 **Superior** PUBLISHING COMPANY

Queen of the Yutana Barge Lines fleet, Tanana *shoves two barges loaded with petroleum products and general cargo along the Yukon River. (Joel W. Rogers)*

FIRST EDITION

Photographic reproduction by Artcraft Colorgraphics, Seattle, WA.
Layout and book design by Phyllis Berg
Typography by Nova Typesetting Co., Bellevue, WA

ACKNOWLEDGEMENTS

This book would not have been possible without the willing cooperation of the rivermen (and women) past and present. Their patient explanation of how things are and their sharing of the way things were is much appreciated. Thank you Duane Benoit, Al Brown, Jack and Bob Coghill, Clyde Day, Jerry Dana, Charlie Hnilicka, Keith Horton, Rick Hoffman, Virgil Patterson, Pat Pedersen, Art and Adriana Peterson, Larry and Artha Shelver and the dozens of others who contributed.

Goetzman-Photo-Davson-

Loading Wood on the Stewart River.

In a scene typical of the steamboat era, the Prospector *takes on a load of cordwood on the Stewart River. The 165-ton vessel was built at Whitehorse in 1901 and operated by the Stewart River Co. and British Yukon Navigation. (University of Alaska)*

DEDICATED

To Larry and Artha Shelver who saw the need and provided their warm support in the compilation of this volume,

and

To Art and Adriana Peterson who nurtured their dream through the pioneer years and watched it come to fruition.

Crew of the Yutana Barge Lines' Kantishna *makes emergency repairs to a bent propeller shaft on the beach at Emmonak in the Yukon Delta. (Fred W. Thomas)*

CONTENTS

Port Captain for Yutana Barge Lines, Allen Brown, directs boatyard crew hauling Tanana *up on the ways for repairs at Nenana, Alaska. (Bob Bune)*

FOREWORD

The history of navigation on the Yukon River system is unlike that of any other river system. The Mississippi and Missouri are bigger and have had more vessels operating on them and for a longer period of time. Other wilderness rivers have developed their own water transportation systems. But nowhere has a wilderness river supported so many boats for such a long period of time.

One may speculate whether, without the Yukon's several gold rushes, navigation would ever have developed at all. Probably not. But the fact is it did develop and forged a permanent interdependency between the residents and commerce of the Interior, particularly of Alaska, the boats and the men who operated them. The airplane and the long-haul tractor-trailer have arrived in the Interior, but they've not doomed the river carriers—merely changed them. And, because they're uniquely adapted to the work required of them, it's likely the Yukon tugs and their barges will be around for some years to come.

There are astonishing elements to the Yukon navigation story. The self-sufficiency of the rivermen is one. From the beginning they not only repaired and completely rebuilt vessels far from any sophisticated shipyard equipment, but they built many boats from scratch right on the beaches and are still doing it.

The fact that these same men would return year after year, pitting themselves against weather, sandbars, wrecks, fires, primitive living conditions and loneliness, for material rewards that were not grand by any means, is also astonishing testimony.

Authorities variously estimate there have been about 250 boats that have plied the Yukon between 1869 and the present. The most complete list of the early boats was put together by William D. MacBride, a freight dispatcher for the British Yukon Navigation Company and founder of the MacBride Museum in Whitehorse. His data covers the period from 1869 to 1914.

The big sternwheelers of the ACC, NCC, NAT & T, BYN, AYN and AAR have taken the glory. But there were all sorts of others—diesel screw, gasoline screw, tunnel boats, even one with six propellers. There were dozens of independent, single-boat or single-launch operators over the years. Some are included here, but because scanty records were kept in the early days, many others have gone unheralded. For this reason, I believe the figure of 250 is conservative and would guess the total number probably approaches 300.

This chronicle attempts to bridge the gap between the sternwheel era (about which much has been written) and the era of modern navigation (about which very little has been written). It also attempts to present the flavor of the rivermen and their work. I have largely ignored historical events that happened elsewhere in the North (the Alaska Pipeline, for example) unless they directly affected Yukon navigation. I have included a brief overview of the geophysical aspects, the Native population and the Klondike because they bear directly on the subject.

Please join me for 114 years of navigation on the Yukon.

I

THE MIGHTY YUKON

Crew and passengers of the steamer S.S. Bailey *pose for a portrait somewhere on the upper Yukon. The* S.S. Bailey *was built on Lake Bennett in 1898, operated on the Bennett-Canyon City run and was taken through the rapids to run between Whitehorse and Dawson. (University of Alaska)*

The Mighty Yukon

The mighty Yukon, fourth largest river in North America, is a river of paradoxes. First major river on this continent to be used by man, it was the last to be discovered by Western civilization. Though its sources rise in tundra and it ends its journey in tundra, it flows through dense boreal forests larger than the state of Texas for most of its course. Once known to nearly every traveler to the interior of Alaska and the Yukon Territory, it's now familiar only to the handful of rivermen who ply its waters and the Native peoples scattered along its banks.

More than a century and a half after its discovery, the Yukon remains untamed, a wilderness river with less than a half dozen highways that even come within sight of it. Except for a few native villages, military bases and two Canadian towns, it's uninhabited for most of its length. Though it has been Alaska's major interior waterway for more than 100 years, it's still uncharted (and unchartable), unmarked by aids to navigation.

The Athabascan Indians gave the river its name which means something akin to "big river." And big it is!

Bracketed by massive mountain ranges—the Coast Mountains and the Alaska Range to the west and south; the Rockies and the Brooks

Range to the east and north—the Yukon swings through a great northward arc that begins less than 15 miles from Pacific salt water and terminates in the Bering Sea. Along the way it ranges through about eight degrees of latitude and 29 of longitude, crosses the Arctic Circle and drains more than 300,000 square miles, an area larger than California, Oregon and Washington that includes more than 52% of the state of Alaska.

Depending on who measures it and where they begin their measurements, the Yukon is variously 1,770 miles long (U.S. Geological Survey; confluence of the Lewes and Pelly Rivers), up to 2,300 miles (Geological Survey of Canada). The generally accepted figure is 1,993 miles, measured from the outlet of Marsh Lake (U.S. Corps of Engineers).

A River of Change

Perhaps the most remarkable feature of the Yukon and its tributaries (and challenge to navigators) is change. As one veteran river pilot put it, "The channel is seldom where you expect to find it and it's certain not to be in the same place it was last week."

For some 40 million years, give or take a couple of million, the Yukon and its tributaries have been flowing westward, carrying what sometimes seems like half of Alaska along with them. Flowing clear, swift and cold from the mountains of western Canada, the river picks up its first major burden of silt at the confluence of the White, just above Dawson. Each tributary contributes thousands of tons of debris until, by the time it reaches central Alaska, a great swath of muddy brown water "too thin to plow and too thick to drink" rolls along at a steady five or six miles per hour.

Swift running on the outside of bends, the water undercuts the soft banks and topples trees to build them up again in the form of sandbars and islands where the current is slack. The result is a nightmare for riverboat skippers. Sandbars lie just beneath the surface waiting to strand even the shallow draft vessels designed for this tricky waterway. Low water in late summer and underwater obstacles that shift with the current make navigation treacherous for even the most experienced.

Land of the midnight sun. Midsummer sun silhouettes George Parks Highway bridge over Tanana River at Nenana. (Fred W. Thomas)

A sudden freeze-up trapped the Vidette *at Indian River, below Dawson, on November 3, 1912. Here, 11 of the 125 passengers and crew haul a lifeboat over the ice to begin the 35-mile trek to Dawson. (Yukon Archives)*

A Short Season

The mountain ranges that define the Yukon's course also determine the climate of its interior basin. Those on the north and east shut the region off from a severe arctic climate; those on the west and south shield it from moist, mild maritime weather. The result is low precipitation (less than 20 inches a year) and great swings in seasonal temperature.

Summers along the Yukon can be the most salubrious the north has to offer with more than 22 hours of daylight in June, temperatures in the 70s, occasionally reaching into the high 80s. (Alaska's maximum temperature record, 100° F, was recorded at Fort Yukon.)

But sublime summers are invariably followed by dreadful winters. The mercury in January and

U.S. Army's steamer General Jefferson C. Davis *is trapped in the ice on the Yukon near Fort Gibbon early in the century. Note the massive blocks of ice that can easily crush a wooden boat to kindling. (Anchorage Historical and Fine Arts Museum)*

The little 50-ton Jennie M *became a victim of the ice at Mt. Romanoff in 1899. Note the shadow of the photographer and his old-fashioned view camera at lower left. (Anchorage Historical and Fine Arts Museum)*

February typically plummets to −30°F to −50°F (a record low of −80°F was recorded at Prospect Creek in 1971).

The result is a very short navigation season. From breakup in mid-May to freeze-up as early as mid-October, vessels can rely on only about four months when the Yukon is ice free. In Norton Sound, at the mouth of the Yukon, the season is even shorter.

Freeze-up can occur gradually over several days with small crystals of ice forming all along the river, then coalescing into small "biscuits" of ice that drift until they meet a sandbar, log or other obstruction to form a barrier from bank to bank. Or, the river can freeze overnight, trapping vessels suddenly.

Woe betide the captain who miscalculates the freeze. Over the years dozens of boats have been

Seattle No. 3 *and* Alaska *frozen in for the winter at Cliff Creek in October 1919. Both vessels were operated by American Yukon Navigation Co. (University of Alaska)*

frozen in, stranded along a lonely stretch far from home port. During the Klondike Gold Rush, prudent skippers refused small fortunes rather than risk their boats in a late season dash upriver to the goldfields.

Spring breakup brings hazard to anything caught in the ice. With a great rending and crashing, hugh flows, some bigger than a small house, grind downstream, crushing anything in their path.

The fate of the steamer *Yukon* is typical.

In the fall of 1946 low water prevented Captain Ralph Newcomb from bringing the Alaska Railroad's wooden sternwheeler back up the Tanana River to her berth at Nenana. She wintered, frozen into the Yukon, at the village of Tanana.

At 2:30 p.m. the following May 12, a great rumble announced the breakup at Tanana. While villagers stood helpless on the bank, great slabs of ice hit the *Yukon* like a juggernaut to drive her up the beach and puncture her sides.

Ice begins moving on the upper river first and, although tributaries such as the Tanana may be ice free early, chunks of drift ice big enough to severely damage a boat remain in the Yukon, preventing navigation into the main river. Ice in Norton Sound typically remains from two to four weeks after the Yukon is clear.

Flooding during breakup is routine. Large ice jams dam the river backing water several feet deep into villages along the bank. Fort Yukon, Rampart, Minto, Nenana, Galena and others have all been submerged over the years.

The annual breakup is reason enough for celebration along the Yukon because it marks the passing of winter and the beginning of a new season of navigation, but it also determines the winners in Alaska's version of a state lottery, the Nenana Ice Pool. Each winter since 1917, thousands of residents (it's only open to residents) have wagered on the exact moment the ice will begin to move in the Tanana River. A line tied to a pylon anchored to the ice in mid-river stops a clock at the instant of movement. In 1982 the breakup occurred at 5:36 p.m. on May 10; three winning tickets split $105,000.

Yutana Barge Lines crew offloads cargo from a barge at Tanana near midnight in July. (Bob Bune)

The Clifford Sifton, *built at Bennett in 1898, owned by a syndicate of Kansas women, shoots Miles Canyon rapids in July 1900. (Anchorage Historical and Fine Arts Museum)*

Canada's Yukon

Though the Yukon technically begins at Marsh Lake, its waters originate on the mountain slopes above Skagway, less than 15 miles from the Pacific. From here rainfall and snow melt flow down through interconnected lakes—Bennett, Tagish, and Marsh—to form the Yukon just above Whitehorse, Yukon Territory.

Seldom more than a mile wide and flanked by steep mountains, these fjord-like lakes are among the loveliest in Canada. All are navigable and steamboats operated on them until replaced by highways after World War II. (The *Tutshi* is preserved intact at Carcross.)

Between Marsh Lake and Whitehorse, the Yukon squeezes through a five mile stretch that includes Miles Canyon, Whitehorse and Squaw Rapids. Now tamed by a dam, whirlpools, huge boulders and standing rapids formed an effective barrier to upriver navigation during the steamboat era and wrecked many a vessel that tried to run them heading downriver.

Whitehorse marked the end of navigation until riverboats ceased operations on the upper Yukon in 1955. Here the steamboats wintered and, at breakup, began their voyages downriver to Dawson and beyond. The last British Yukon Navigation Company (a White Pass and Yukon subsidiary) sternwheeler, the *Klondike*, is permanently moored at Whitehorse as a Parks Canada museum.

Just below the city, the Yukon flows into Lake Laberge, famous as the site of Robert Service's "Cremation of Sam McGee." Laberge usually remains frozen for two weeks or more after the river ice has gone out and presented problems to captains who wanted to get an early start downriver. By pouring a combination of oil and lampblack in a path across the ice, they induced enough melting to enable a steamer to move through it.

From Laberge to the old North West Mounted Police Post at Hootalinqua, a distance of 30

The Dawson, *a British Yukon Navigation Co. boat on the Whitehorse-Dawson run, picks her way through Five Finger Rapids in 1905. (Yukon Archives)*

miles, the Yukon was once called (and is still locally known as) the Thirty Mile River. Icy waters run clear and swift here as it winds through canyons carved by the wind into grotesque rock formations. The broad Teslin, first of the Yukon's major tributaries, flows 253 miles out of the Cassiar Mountains to confluence at Hootalinqua.

The decaying remains of several sternwheelers litter the river downstream from the Teslin. Some were beached and abandoned; others were wrecked on submerged rocks. The 508-ton *Norcom* (ex-*Evelyn*, 1908) lies rotting on Shipyard Island. The *Klondike* (II) crashed into a rock cliff at the lower end of Thirty Mile in 1936 and promptly sank.

Five Finger Rapids, where the river divides into five channels around four islands, was another treacherous stretch for paddlewheelers. The channels are so narrow and the water so swift, transportation companies anchored a permanent cable along the bank and boats winched themselves through the rapids. Five Finger and Rink Rapids claimed several victims over the years. The *Dawson* went down in 1926 and the *Casca* (II) ten years later.

Fort Selkirk, 282 miles below Whitehorse, marks the confluence of the 457-mile Pelly River. One of the earliest settlements on the river, it was founded in 1848 as a trading post of the Hudson's Bay Company.

The aptly named White, with its great burden

The White Horse, *nicknamed "The Old Gray Mare", negotiates tricky Five Finger Rapids in 1905. The rapids are named for five channels that course around four rocky islands in the Yukon. (University of Alaska)*

of silt from the St. Elias Range, and the Stewart enter the Yukon within a few miles of each other. Steamboats plied the Stewart for many years, hauling gold and silver ore from mines at Mayo and transferring their loads to larger Yukon boats at Stewart Island.

Dawson, heart of the Klondike, was important to the steamboats as a major terminus or stop-over point. Vessels beat their way upriver from St. Michael, downriver from Whitehorse and furnished local service in between. The *Keno* (1937), one of the Stewart River ore steamers, is beached on the riverbank as a museum here and there's a graveyard of disintegrating boats just downriver from the town.

In the next 300 miles, the Yukon flows through a wilderness country (much of it incorporated in Yukon-Charley and Yukon Flats National Monuments), punctuated here and there by former mining camps, trading posts and Indian villages. Low hills and bluffs of the Yukon-Tanana highlands flank the river. Steamboats regularly stopped at Forty-Mile, Eagle, Coal and Woodchopper Creeks, Star and Nation to unload freight and mail or replenish wood supplies. Eagle, the first village on the Alaska side of the border, served for many years as a customs post for vessels bound downriver.

The Middle Yukon

From a point near Circle, past Fort Yukon and the confluence of the Porcupine River, to beyond Stevens Village (some 250 miles), the Yukon spreads out in a maze of channels, islands, sandbars, sloughs, potholes, marshes and ponds known as Yukon Flats. An underlying layer of permafrost, saturated soil and low gradient give this 11,000 square mile area the character of one vast swamp.

Early explorers spent days picking their way through the confusing waterways. During the steamboat era, boats headed downriver picked up a pilot at Circle to lead them through channels that moved daily. (Yutana Barge Lines still uses pilots scouting ahead of its tugs in outboards.) Strandings were common. Typical is the experience of the *Yukon* that spent five days with a full complement of passengers languishing on a sandbar in the 1920s. In 1897 more than 2,500 Klondike-bound miners spent the winter at Circle and elsewhere on the river when their sternwheelers were stranded by autumn low water and freeze-up.

The same soggy landscape that makes the river a nightmare for navigators is a paradise for wildlife. Yukon Flats is one of North America's most important waterfowl habitats with

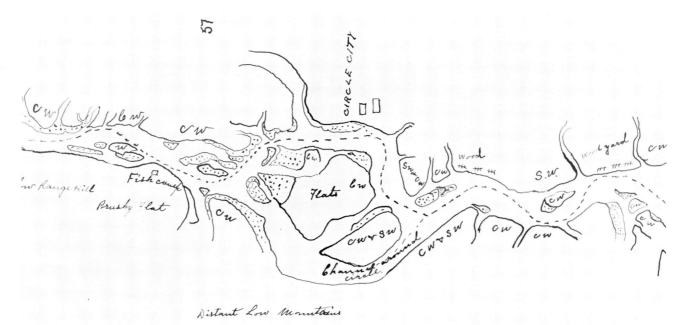

Hand-drawn chart of the Yukon typical of the "personal" charts made by pilots around the turn of the century shows sections of the river around Circle City, Fort Yukon and White Eye. Never previously published, the chart was the property of Captain John Fussell, drawn by his wife, Agnes Fussell, and used on AYN and BYN vessels. Even today, pilots must use primitive charts such as this one for there are no official charts of the river. (Anchorage Historical and Fine Arts Museum)

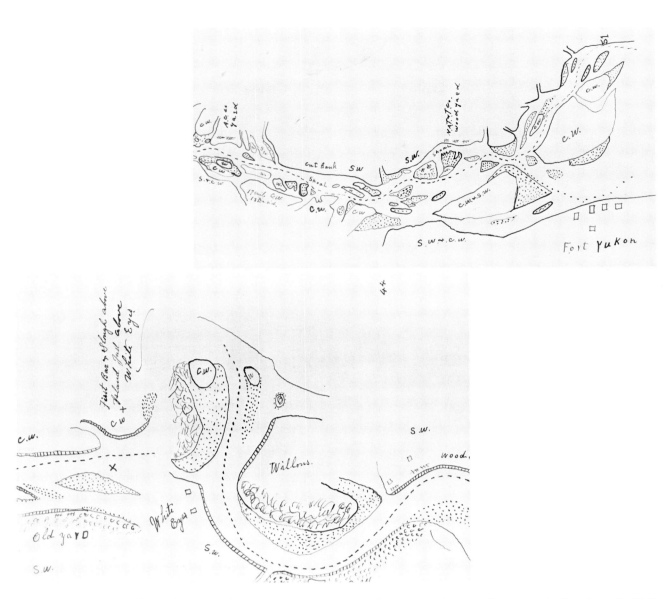

more than two million ducks and geese in residence each summer, plus scores of other species including eagles, ospreys, hawks and falcons. Two large caribou herds graze in the flats; there are moose, bear, wolves and smaller animals as well.

All this standing water breeds hordes of mosquitoes. The plague of rivermen, they're often wryly referred to as Alaska's state bird.

At Fort Yukon, eight miles north of the Arctic Circle, the river reaches its northern limit and swings southwestward for the Bering Sea. The original fort was founded as a Hudson's Bay fur trading post in 1847, went on to become an important riverboat stop and trading center for the Northern Commercial Company. Today the town is the largest Alaskan community on the Yukon (population about 700), the site of a U.S. Air Force installation and the upper limit of commercial navigation.

Athabascan villages of White Eye, Beaver, Purgatory, Stevens Village and Rampart, none of them numbering more than 100 souls, perch on the banks of the river beyond Fort Yukon. Just west of Stevens Village, the North Slope Haul Road crosses the river on the only bridge across Alaska's Yukon. At Rampart, the river cuts through steep slopes to form Rampart Gorge, once proposed as the site of a massive dam that would have submerged the village and flooded the valley far upstream into the Yukon Flats.

Though at 513 miles it's not the longest tributary, the Tanana is by far the most important. Even before the discovery of gold in 1902, pad-

19

dle-wheelers ascended the muddy Tanana and its tributary, the Chena, to a point near present-day Fairbanks. With the completion of the Alaska Railroad in 1923, Nenana, on the south bank of the Tanana, became the most important trans-shipment point on the Yukon system. Freight, mail and passengers brought from Seward and Anchorage by rail were loaded on the riverboats at Nenana for points in the interior.

After the Klondike Gold Rush, boats coming downstream from Whitehorse and Dawson and upstream from St. Michael made Nenana their terminus or turn-around point. Smaller vessels departed from here to ply side streams such as the Kantishna. Today, Nenana is headquarters and home port for Yutana Barge Lines, the single major carrier remaining on the river.

The shallow Tanana has always been troublesome for rivermen. Low water and a sandy bottom combine to build islands and constantly shifting sandbars near its mouth, particularly around a notorious stretch known as Squaw Crossing.

Nearly level for miles, rounded into low mountains in places, the land bordering the middle Yukon and its tributaries, to within about 250 miles of salt water, is covered in swampy muskeg and forest so thick it's nearly impossible for a man to penetrate it. Birch, aspen, spruce, balsam, cottonwood, larch and tamarack carpet the hillsides and grow right to the water's edge. By mid-September the deciduous trees, especially birch and aspen, splash the landscape with great swaths of gold.

Because of the trees, the Russians named this type of country *taiga* or "land of little sticks." Seldom over 20 feet tall, many of them, particularly the black spruce, are more than 200 years old, stunted by the harsh climate. The spruce provided steamboats with a limitless supply of

Aerial view of the Tanana River about 60 miles below Nenana, between Minto and Tolovana. Note extensive sandbars. (Bob Bune)

The Suzie, *elegant sternwheeler of Mississippi River packetboat design, lends assistance to* Seattle No. 3 *that appears to be stranded on a sandbar. (University of Alaska)*

cordwood, but also posed occasional hazards to navigation when, their roots undercut by the river, they hung out over the channel to become "sweepers." A sweeper could easily punch holes in wooden deck houses or knock an unwary deckhand right into the river.

In addition to abundant moose, bear, fox, lynx, coyote and rabbit, the river valleys are populated with commercially valuable fur bearing animals—muskrat, beaver, otter, mink, marten and ermine. A bonanza for early trappers, they still produce a harvest of about $6 million annually.

Below the Tanana, the Yukon still has another 720 miles to reach the Bering Sea. Flowing past riverfront villages at Tanana, Ruby, Galena, Koyukuk, Nulato, Kalteg, Grayling, Holy Cross, Russian Mission and Marshall, the river provided the only highway to the outside for uncounted generations until air service opened up the interior during the 1920s and '30s. Even today no roads connect these villages with the rest of Alaska.

Galena, one of the larger river communities, is the location of the U.S. Military airbase closest to the Soviet Union, home for supersonic fighters that fly "top cover" against potential intruders from beyond the Bering Strait. Just downstream, the Koyukuk, flowing 554 miles southwestward from the Brooks Range, adds its waters to the Yukon. This river, the Yukon's second longest tributary (after the Porcupine), once supported an active steamboat trade that reached as far as Bettles.

The Delta

Loaded with tremendous quantities of silt, sand, gravel and other debris for most of its course, the river finally deposits its burden in a vast fan-shaped delta that stretches 250 miles across (including the delta of the neighboring Kuskokwim River) and reaches inland for 200 miles to the base of the Kuskokwim Mountains. The volume of solids is awesome. In a single year the Yukon dumps more than 100 million metric tons in the delta and the river's sediment "plume" extends over 4,000 square miles into the Bering Sea.

Like Yukon Flats and the mouth of the Tanana, the delta is one great headache for navigators. A maze of false and shifting channels, sloughs and backwaters makes it tricky to negotiate even with the shallow draft vessels designed for these waters. Dense fogs, strong onshore winds and changing tides that periodically blanket the landscape compound the problem.

Clara Hickman Rust, writing of her voyage upriver as a passenger aboard the sternwheeler *Suzie* in 1908, described a typical delta stranding:

> "... we were left high and dry as the tide went out. The range of tide here is only a couple of feet or so, but the channel is shallow at best, and with the river so low there was just not enough water to float us and our barges. Moreover, because the wind has a good deal of effect on the tide here, the captain said it might be as long as 48 hours before we floated. ... the next morning we found that the *Suzie* was not alone in her predicament. Four other boats were downstream from us, their smoke stacks standing out against the rosy morning sky."

Lack of standing timber was another problem steamboats faced. The delta is treeless and the boats either had to carry enough cordwood on their downriver trip to get them to St. Michael and back to wood supplies or they had to rely on driftwood, which was abundant in the early days but became scare as more and more boats consumed it. Some boats were converted to burn oil for just this reason.

The Yukon has two main entry channels—the south, or Alakanuk Channel, and the north, or Apoon Channel. Most vessels use the Apoon Channel.

There's no deep water, no shelter from storms and no place that could remotely be classified as a proper harbor in the delta so transportation companies were forced to use the barely adequate harbor at St. Michael, about 50 miles up the coast. Though the harbor is too shallow for any but the shallow-draft riverboats and barges to tie up along the shore, deep-draft ocean going ships could (and still do) anchor in the roadstead and transfer inbound cargoes and passengers.

Covered with grass, sedges and standing water, the flat landscape of the delta makes another ideal habitat for bird populations. Millions of geese, ducks, swans and shorebirds nest here each summer. Small mammals such as muskrat, mink and beaver live along the waterways and ocean mammals, particularly seals and beluga whales, swim into the river.

But the real treasure is the horde of sleek, silvery salmon that enter the delta each summer and fall, swimming up the Yukon and its tributaries to spawn. The single most important food source on the river, salmon has provided sustenance for the Native peoples and their dogs since the beginning, plus the basis of commerce with the outside world. Chum and king salmon are the most abundant, but the river also hosts several runs of sockeye, coho and pink salmon. In the early 1900s, when the first records of such things were kept, the harvest often exceeded two million annually.

II

THE FIRST ALASKANS

Prior to the building of the Alaska Railroad, Indian salmon fishing camps like this one occupied the riverbanks at Nenana during the summer months. (University of Alaska)

The First Alaskans

No one knows when the first Indian sighted the Yukon River. No one knows when he caught his first salmon, brought down his first caribou or when he discovered that sheltering in a covered hole in the ground protected him from the harsh winter climate.

But we do know how he got there.

During the Pleistocene epoch that ended about 11,000 years ago, the great ice sheets that covered a great deal of North America locked up much of the earth's water, lowering ocean levels. Alaska was connected to Siberia by an exposed land bridge nearly 1,000 miles wide.

Most archaeologists agree that at least 15,000 years ago the forebears of Alaska's Indians (and indeed most of the Native peoples of the Americas) trekked across the land bridge following game animals. As retreating glaciers freed the valley of the Yukon, it served as a natural highway that led them gradually, after many successive generations, to penetrate the interior, cross into what is now Canada and migrate southward to warmer climes, as well as settle along the coast and Aleutian chain.

The Athabascans

The Athabascan Indians (sometimes spelled Athapascan) of Alaska's interior were a semi-nomadic people. Dependent on fish and game, they moved with the caribou and salmon, seldom settling in any one place for very long. The basic social unit was a nuclear family that occasionally

This photograph of an Indian family living on the Yukon was probably taken about 1900. Note Russian-style fur hat on boy second from right. (Yukon Archives)

Wisdom and the knowledge of many years spent hunting along the Kuskokwim River are etched in the face of this patriarch of Kalskag village. (Bob Bune)

Eskimo matriarch of Stebbins, a village at the mouth of the Yukon, weaves baskets in a generations-old traditional style. (Bob Bune)

Finely crafted Eskimo basket is fashioned of tightly woven tundra grasses formed in a coil with an inner lining of grass woven at right angles. (Bob Bune)

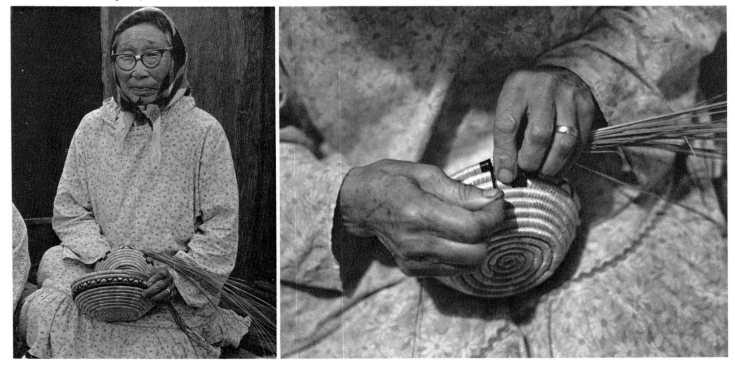

came together with other such families at summer fish camps or winter quarters. Poor land could not support large settlements and the Indian villages we know today along the Yukon are a relatively modern phenomenon. Like the white man who followed them, they traveled along the river, seldom straying very far into the impenetrable forests on either side.

Though they didn't form tribes as other North American Indians did, they were divided into six basic language groupings defined by spoken dialect. The Ingaliks occupied the westernmost section of the Yukon where they encountered the Eskimo culture some 250 miles from the coast. The Koyukons were located around what is now Nulato and the Koyukuk River valley; the Tananas were in the central Yukon; the Kutchin in the Yukon Flats area; the Han upstream near Eagle and the Tutchone in the Canadian Yukon.

When the first white men encountered the Athabascans in the mid-19th century, they were a classic Stone Age hunting and gathering people whose lifestyle had probably not changed much in thousands of years. They had no written language. They hunted with spears and arrows tipped with caribou bone, caught small animals and birds in traps and snares and fished for grayling, salmon and other fish by means of nets and traps. If the summer harvest was bountiful, there was enough smoked fish and meat to tide them over the winter; if not, they were forced to continue hunting (and moving) through the long icy winter.

In explaining why the Athabascans did not develop the intricate culture and fine arts common to the coastal tribes, Archie Satterfield in his book, *After the Gold Rush*, speculates:

"... they were a people who never had enough to eat. Their whole lives were devoted to food gathering, and there is grim evidence of frequent famines and occasional forays into cannibalism."

In winter villages the Indians built a variety of dwellings ranging from the semi-sunken homes covered with earth near the coast (a design borrowed from the neighboring Eskimos) to log or pole houses covered with animal hides further inland. Women and children lived in small houses where the women spent the winter sewing clothing from hides and sinew, making baskets,

Typical Indian encampment for summer salmon fishing along the Yukon, probably between 1902 and 1910. (Yukon Archives)

weaving snowshoe webbing, making nets, caulking birch bark canoes and cooking.

The men of the village spent their time in a larger structure, the *kashim*, making sleds, canoes, lamps, arrow and spearheads and a host of other Stone Age implements. Similar to the *kiva* used by the Pueblo Indians of the southwest (also Athabascans); the *kashim* was a prehistoric fraternal lodge and health spa as much as it was a dwelling. Here the men sat around a large smoky fire, sweating profusely and bathing themselves from time to time in bowls of urine.

The Nulato Massacre

Indian folklore tells of fighting between themselves and between Indians and Eskimos in prehistoric times but, unlike their cousins, the Plains Indians, they have been generally peaceful since the arrival of the white man, even though he threatened their traditional hunting and fishing grounds. There is at least one notable exception.

In 1841 the Russians established a fur trading post at Nulato that, a decade later, had become their most important post on the Yukon and the limit of their penetration upriver. The post was run by a cruel trader, Vasili Deriabin, with a reputation for abusing the Indians. That February of 1851 Lieutenant John J. Bernard of the British Royal Navy's *H.M.S. Enterprise* also happened to be at the post where he had stopped to winter in his search for the survivors of the ill-fated Sir John Franklin exploration party.

The local Nulato band of Koyukon Indians had traditionally raided another band living upriver and in the early morning hours of February 16 the upriver band retaliated. Trapping nearly 100 Nulatos in three large subterranean houses, they set the houses afire, shooting any with arrows who tried to get out through the burning walls. Only a handful of women and children escaped.

At the nearby post the Russians were unaware of the massacre when one of the attackers fell upon Deriabin, stabbing him to death. A Russian interpreter who had come to the rescue fell in a hail of arrows. Seizing Bernard in his bed, they delivered a mortal stab wound to his stomach, from which he succumbed several days later.

Next attacking workmen in their barracks (who, by this time, were forewarned), the Indians were driven off with accurate rifle fire from inside the building. Thus ended what has come to be

known as the Nulato massacre, the only skirmish of any size to take place between the whites and the Athabascans.

The Eskimos

Migrating to the Bering coast between 10,000 and 15,000 years ago, the Arctic-Mongoloid peoples of Siberia, who evolved into today's Eskimos and Aleuts, arrived sometime after the Indians. Yup'ik Eskimos who settled in the Yukon-Kuskokwim Delta discovered a home that, though harsh, was rich in fish and game most years. Their culture never penetrated very far inland and today meets the Indian culture along the Yukon at the village of Holy Cross.

Like their Indian cousins, they were hunters, but because of the availability of food and the relative ease of travel were probably less nomadic. Villages grew up around fish, bird and animal habitats, where hunters from traditionally nuclear families banded together to pursue whales and other marine mammals.

Their skin-covered kayaks made it easy to travel on the lakes, sloughs and streams of the delta during the summer. During the winter clear, treeless ice and snow provided good routes for travel by snowshoe and later by dog team and sled.

When the first explorers reached the Yukon they encountered Indians such as this one fishing from canoes with dip nets. Photo taken about 1898. (University of Alaska)

Eskimo youngster from St. Michael trudges through waist-high marsh grass that covers much of the Yukon Delta. Note headband from Iditerod sled-dog race. (Barry C. Anderson)

Drying racks loaded with salmon line the banks of the Yukon at the village of Tanana. Tanana discharges cargo in the background. (Barry C. Anderson)

Fish, especially salmon, was the staple food for both man and dog. Caught in the river and estuary, it was dried or smoked to stock larders over the winter. When the opportunity arose, the Eskimos hunted for seal, whale and occasionally walrus and, venturing away from the tundra, they brought down some moose, caribou and bear. When big game was not available or the salmon run was poor, they supplemented their diet with small mammals—otter, muskrat, mink—and the abundant geese and ducks in the delta.

Like the Indians, the Eskimos used virtually every part of the animal. Hides went for shelter, clothing and boat covers; sealskin for mukluks; sinew for sewing and snowshoe webbing, bone for needles, spear and arrow points.

The Eskimos and Indians share a reverence for the land and its animals that has evolved into an intertwining of animal and spirit in folklore. Fish bones are returned to the river and animal bones to the forest so that, from them, new fish and animals may arise. The raven, a foremost spirit, is credited with carving out the Yukon-Kuskokwim Delta with his talons.

Another tradition shared by both peoples (as well as the coastal Indians of southeastern Alaska, British Columbia and the Pacific Northwest states) is the potlatch. Usually held to honor the dead, the potlatch is characterized by extensive gift giving by the host and his relatives. The gift giver gained respect in proportion to the amount and value of the gift and, in many instances, gave away all that he owned. Potlatches sometimes lasted for weeks with hundreds of guests who danced, feasted and related tales for days on end. The missionaries tried to stamp out the practice and the British Columbia

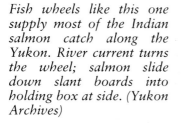
Fish wheels like this one supply most of the Indian salmon catch along the Yukon. River current turns the wheel; salmon slide down slant boards into holding box at side. (Yukon Archives)

government outlawed it in the 1920s, but potlatches are still given occasionally along the Yukon where guests come for miles and stay for days.

A Clash of Cultures

Fish wheels still turn quietly on the Yukon and its tributaries and the fish they trap still hang drying on the riverbanks, but in the village store the shelves are lined with cans of Coke, bottles of Joy and containers of home permanent preparation.

The white man's culture has had a tremendous impact on the millenia-old Native culture and not all of it is good. The fish wheel (a white man's invention) and the rifle have replaced the net and the arrow, but the game is disappearing. The motorboat and snowmobile are replacing the canoe and dog team, but gasoline costs money and there are no jobs. There are hospitals to treat diseases the white man brought. There are schools that teach English, but few Natives under 25 are fluent in the language of their parents and grandparents.

The potlatch is the traditional Indian gift-giving celebration throughout the northern tribes. These men are gathered for one held at Eagle in 1907. (Yukon Archives)

During the steamboat era, Indians supplied cordwood from camps such as this one on the upper Yukon. Date of photo is July 1900. (Yukon Archives)

The change began with the first traders. The Eskimos and Indians for generations had existed in a subsistence economy; i.e., the hunter caught what he needed for his family to survive. Only the most personal property was considered private; any disused equipment reverted to those who had need of it.

Suddenly, the furs he trapped had value beyond what was necessary to keep him warm. He bartered them to the Russians for trade goods—beads, metal, axes, pots and pans. The transition to a commercial economy had been made.

With the coming of the steamboats, vast quantities of wood were needed for the voracious boilers and many Indians were employed cutting hundreds of cords of wood. Others became deckhands or pilots on the boats where they gained a reputation for keen eyes and good judgment. Even today, Yutana Barge Lines' most proficient pilot is an Indian, Dave Walker, who makes his home in Holy Cross.

From time to time, spurts of military construction employ some natives. Some still trap for furs. And, a resurgence of the commercial salmon industry in the delta in recent years has brought a livelihood to some of the Eskimos living there.

But, in general, there has been no sustained economic base on which to build a new lifestyle. Unemployment runs more than 90% in many villages, while most are receiving welfare and food stamps.

The Native Villages

St. Michael is typical of coastal villages. Once a booming gold rush port with a population that

Venerable Eskimo hunter at St. Michael has just re-
turned from a sealing expedition in Norton Sound.
Today's Natives use power boats and modern
weapons, but continue to hunt in the traditional
manner. (Bob Bune)

Two giggly little Eskimo girls posed for their portrait
at Alakunuk, a delta village. (Bob Bune)

Eskimo residences at St. Michael are primitive, without running water or sewers, but most boast color
television sets and receive programs by satellite. (Fred W. Thomas)

BEAVER
31F507

Until recent years. Indians served as skilled pilots aboard the Yukon stern-wheelers and tugs. Jimmy Huntington (shown here aboard the Beaver on the Koyukuk River) went on to become a leading legislator in the Alaska state government. (Arthur Peterson)

Delighted Eskimo family poses aboard their new all-terrain vehicle at St. Michael. Natives use these three-wheeled cycles to scoot across the tundra in summer. (Bob Bune)

reached 10,000, St. Michael now has 283 residents, 95% of whom are Eskimo. Modest wooden houses line the beach along a wooden boardwalk above tundra that is swampy in the summertime (permafrost is one to three feet below the surface) and frozen hard in the winter. Two small stores, one owned by the Alaska Commercial Company, the other by the Tachik Native Corporation, purvey groceries that are brought in by airplane. The Bureau of Indian Affairs operates a sizable school and during the summer the bureau's ship *North Star III* calls at the village.

There are no cars or trucks for St. Michael is on an island, but three-wheeled all-terrain vehicles buzz up and down the boardwalk in the summer; snowmobiles cross the snow and frozen bay in the winter. There is no running water; villagers carry it by bucket from a community supply. There are no sewers or garbage services; refuse is dumped in pits in summer and on the ice of the bay in winter.

And, except for the handful that work for the petroleum distributor, the school, the stores or, in the summer, for Black Navigation, there are no jobs. Nearly every family is on welfare. But the village does have one new luxury—a big white dish antenna that brings TV to every home that can afford a set.

Oil exploration in Norton Sound, if successful, could result in prosperity once again for St. Michael. Because it has the only harbor anywhere in the area, drilling and production companies may use it as a base.

Galena, on the other hand, is relatively affluent by YukonRiver Standards. The Air Force base as well as Wein and the other regional air carriers provide jobs as well as closer contact with the outside. Though most homes do not have sewers and running water, things are changing with an infusion of federal dollars to build new homes on high ground away from the flooding that periodically plagues Galena.

Alaska Native Claims Settlement Act

The Alaska Native Claims Settlement Act of 1971 made giant strides in making natives full participants in the white man's economy and no longer wards of the government. The act conveyed title to 40 million acres of land previously held by the Federal government and awarded compensation amounting to $962.5 million, of which $462.5 million was to be paid from the national treasury and the remainder from mineral revenue sharing.

But in addition to conveying land ownership to villages and individuals, the act provided for 12 regional native corporations to compete in the white man's economy. Every person with ¼ or more Eskimo, Indian or Aleut blood was entitled to shares of stock in the new corporations. Though it's still too early to determine the ultimate success or failure of this venture into private enterprise, the corporations have already invested in a wide variety of income-producing projects including fishing boats, hotels, housing developments, service and trucking firms, bank shares and petroleum and gas exploration companies.

III

DISCOVERY AND EXPLORATION
1833-1896

Anvik was one of the early Christian missions established on the lower Yukon, just above Holy Cross. Note primitive wooden tanks on barge that carried fuel oil for steamboats operating in the delta. (University of Alaska)

Discovery and Exploration
1833–1896

For nearly a century after Vitus Bering discovered Alaska and claimed it for Russia in 1741, the Yukon River remained unknown, to any but the Eskimos and Indians. During those years the Russian-American Company had been busy developing a lucrative fur trade along Alaska's Pacific shores from headquarters in Sitka.

Having depleted the once-rich resources of sea otter and fur seal along the easily accessible stretches of coast, Aleutians and Pribiloffs, the Russians reached further north to the Bering Sea coast. In 1833 Lieutenant Michael Tebenkov established a fortified outpost, Redoubt St. Michael, on St. Michael Island some 50 miles north of the great river the Eskimos called Kuikpak, the present-day Yukon.

Within the year the Russians were moving inland. Andrei Glazunov, traveling overland by dog sled in the company of five other Russians and three natives, reached the Indian village of Anvik on the Yukon in 1834. By 1837 the Russians had established a fur trading post at the present site of Russian Mission and another at Nulato in 1838. Lieutenant L.A. Zagoskin of the Russian Navy followed in 1842, ascending the river as far as the mouth of the Tanana. He declared the Yukon unnavigable beyond this point, a report which may have discouraged Russian exploration further upriver.

So far as is known, these Russian expeditions traveled mostly in the winter using dog teams and snowshoes. When they ventured onto the river, they probably used Indian canoes or constructed their own. The dawn of Yukon navigation would wait another 27 years.

But the Russians did not have the river to themselves for long. British traders of the Hudson's Bay Company, having established a string of trading posts across the wilds of Canada, were pushing westward.

Accompanied by a French-Canadian voyageur and two Indians, Robert Campbell crossed the Rockies and discovered the headwaters of the Pelly (and thus the Yukon) in the summer of 1840, but returned eastward the same year.

The near impossibility of communication across the vast stretches of wilderness is amply illustrated by the events of 1847 and 1848. John Bell, employed by the Hudson's Bay Company, crossed the Rockies and descended the Porcupine; Alexander Murray built the first post at Fort Yukon in 1847. The following year, ignorant of the location of Murray's post, Campbell returned to the Pelly and built an HBC post at Fort Selkirk at the confluence of the Yukon. Later in the year, he and his party continued another 500 miles downriver to discover the HBC flag already flying over a fort on the same river.

The Arrival of the Americans

A series of events in 1867 were to have a great impact on the future of the Yukon.

The first, the American Telegraph Expedition, though an exercise in futility, was responsible for the first detailed reconnaissance and mapping of the river. The Russians and British, entrenched at either end of the river, had not met, though each knew of the other's presence through information supplied by the Indians.

In 1865 Major Robert Kennicott, the only American who had ever seen the Yukon, was appointed to survey a route for the American portion of a transcontinental telegraph. The proposed route would span 6,000 miles through British Columbia, interior Alaska and cross the Bering Strait to Siberia, thus linking the United States with Europe.

Kennicott brought with him the tiny steamboat, *Lizzie-Horner*, that would have been the first steamboat on the Yukon had it not been for mechanical problems that prevented its use.

The expedition was delayed by Kennicott's untimely death, but did get underway in command of William Healey Dall in the spring of 1867. Towing and paddling canoes against the current, they made their way up to Fort Yukon. Two members of the party—Frank Ketchum and Mike Laberge (for whom Lake Laberge is named)—journeyed as far upriver as the confluence of the Pelly.

Unfortunately, the party returned jubilantly downriver, having successfully completed their survey to find the project had been scrapped in favor of a newly laid Atlantic cable.

The United States purchased Alaska from Russia in 1867. Concurrently, the Russian-American Company sold warehouses, trading posts, ships and inventories to the American firm of Hutchinson Kohl & Company. Within a year, the name was changed to Alaska Commercial Company (ACC), an enterprise that was to account for most of the Alaska fur trade, most of the commercial trade on the Yukon and was to extend a network of trading posts that blanketed the territory for nearly a century.

Commercial Navigation Begins

In June 1869, the ACC ship *Commodore* arrived at St. Michael carrying on her deck a diminutive 50-foot sternwheeler, *Yukon*, destined to be the first steamboat on the river. With flags flying and guns firing, the little steamer left St. Michael on July 4 under the command of Captain Benjamin Hall. Picking her way through channels that had never before been navigated by anything larger than a canoe, she reached Nulato 16 days later and Fort Yukon on July 31.

Aboard the *Yukon* on this first voyage was Captain Charles P. Raymond, U.S. Army, sent by the government to determine the international boundary between the Alaska Territory and Canada's Yukon Territory. Reaching Fort Yukon, he discovered the Hudson's Bay Company operating 80 miles inside U.S. territory. Raising the American flag over the fort, he took possession for the U.S.

All during the 1870s, the *Yukon* was the only commercial vessel on the river. Each summer she carried supplies upriver to trading posts, trappers and prospectors as far up as the Stewart and Pelly Rivers, returning with bundles of furs and ore samples. Company agent Leroy McQuesten sometimes acted as captain as well as fireman, engineer, mechanic and pilot and was the only white man aboard. He related, "It is a wonder to me that we didn't blow her up or sink her as I didn't know anything about steamboating. Often

This wooden Russian Orthodox church, topped by the traditional onion domes, and its graveyard still stand at Kalskag on the Kuskokwim River. (Bob Bune)

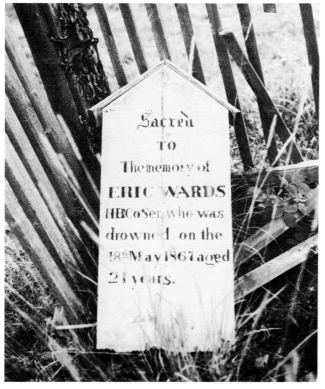

Many of the young adventurers who sought adventure on the northern frontier never returned to their homeland. This grave commemorates a young Hudson's Bay Company employee. (Henry S. Kaiser, Jr.)

Russian cemetery at St. Michael is studded with ornate Russian Orthodox crosses that mark graves of those who perished in the service of the Russian-American (Fur) Company. (Bob Bune)

we would get a moose in the water and all hands would grab the guns and let the steamer take care of herself."

On one voyage in 1874, the *Yukon* deposited McQuesten, an assistant and a load of trade goods just upstream from a river the Indians called Trundeck. They were to establish a new post, Fort Reliance, the most distant from St. Michael at the time. The river they called the Trundeck would later become famous as the Klondike.

In 1879, a competing company, the Western Fur and Trading Company, brought a second sternwheeler to the river, the 28-ton *St. Michael* under the command of Captain P.M. Anderson.

Since the discovery of gold near Juneau in 1880, prospectors were reaching the Yukon in increasing numbers. Though they found "color" along some of the tributaries (principally the Tanana and Stewart), the big strikes were still a half dozen years away.

One of these adventurers was Edward Schieffelin, fresh from making his first fortune in the bonanza at Tombstone, Arizona. Shieffelin and his party didn't stay long, but they did bring with them another steamer, the *New Racket*. With her

small hull occupied almost entirely by boiler and engine, she was reputed to be the ugliest vessel ever to ply the Yukon. Leaking steam from every joint and belching an exhaust that could be heard for miles, she lived up to her rather unusual name. When Shieffelin left, he sold her to three ACC employees that included Leroy McQuesten.

Ironically, both the first and third steamboats also became the first victims of ice. The *Yukon*, after wintering in a slough near Fort Yukon, was crushed to kindling. *New Racket* suffered a similar fate.

The First Strikes

With all of the prospecting going on along the Yukon River system, it was inevitable the seekers would find gold in respectable quantities sooner or later. In the summer of 1885 Harry Madison and Howard Franklin were sinking holes in the muskeg 23 miles up the Forty Mile River when they retrieved a handful of nuggets, some as large as a thumbnail. By fall miners already on the Stewart had moved downstream to the new diggings. With the spring thaw others trekked in over Chilcoot Pass. By 1890 Forty Mile had become the largest settlement on the Yukon, a

Spare interior of this mission church welcomes Native worshippers even today. (Henry S. Kaiser, Jr.)

boom town of about 200 cabins, six saloons, two blacksmith shops, stores and an opera house featuring San Francisco dance hall girls.

For the first few summers after the Forty Mile strike the two steamboats were unequal to the task of supplying several hundred miners with enough food to last the winter. More than two-thirds of the camp's population was forced to go downriver to St. Michael or over Chilcoot Pass to spend the winter, returning the following spring.

To meet the increasing demand for river transportation, ACC built a new steamboat, *Arctic*, at St. Michael in 1889. Big by pre-Klondike standards, she measured 135 by 30 feet. Scarcely had she got underway on her first voyage than the fickle winds of Norton Sound drove her on the rocks where she immediately sank. Though she was refloated and repaired and operated the following year, cancellation of her maiden season left many a hungry miner at Forty Mile during the winter of 1889. In 1896, the *Arctic* became the first riverboat to reach the new settlement of Dawson and was wrecked in the breakup at Circle City the following spring.

New Blood Comes to the River

In 1891 a group of Chicago investors, including Michael Cudahy of the famous meat packing family, formed a new company, North American Transportation & Trading, to break ACC's monopoly of the Yukon trade. The following year NAT&T constructed a new steamer, the *Portus B. Weare*, at St. Michael, from materials freighted from San Francisco. Now the largest on the river, the *P.B. Weare* measured 175 by 28 feet and carried 230 horsepower engines. She began her career in 1893 when the company opened its first trading post at Forty Mile.

By the mid-1880s, St. Michael was enjoying a mini boom of its own. Alaska Commercial Company occupied the old Russian fort from which it supplied goods for the steamers going upriver to its trading posts and whatever natives, prospectors, trappers or missionaries happened to be on hand. The village had grown to include a small hotel, warehouses, shipways and docks.

But though it had gained some measure of civilization, "St. Mike" was still a bleak and barren place. As one traveler from San Francisco who arrived there in 1884 remarked: "There may be causes why certain people should come to Alaska and settle, as there have been arguments for making penal colonies in the Aleutian Archipelago. But the reason for the one must be that the immigrants were personal enemies of those who advised their removal, and for the other that starvation should be the lot of all criminals."

In 1893 another rich strike on Birch Creek, some 140 miles below Forty Mile, led to the founding of Circle City. Between 1894 and 1896 the population grew to more than a thousand miners producing more than $1 million in gold annually. In addition to hundreds of log cabins, the rough and tumble town included 27 saloons and eight dance halls.

New towns meant new ships and in 1895 ACC added two sternwheelers to their expanding fleet. The *Alice* was a 400-ton vessel and the *Bella* a bit smaller at 370 tons. Both were built on the ways at St. Michael.

These first Yukon riverboats were primitive affairs, designed primarily for cargo carrying. Miners, missionaries and trappers who traveled on them were often required to supply their own sleeping gear and food and frequently slept on deck. As passenger traffic increased, the newer boats were built with inside cabins and began carrying much of the freight lashed to one or two barges pushed ahead of the prime mover.

Just four major sternwheelers—*P.B. Weare*, *Arctic*, *Alice* and *Bella*—were operating on the Yukon on the eve of the greatest gold strike the north has ever known. Within the next decade their ranks would be multiplied many fold.

IV

GOLD FEVER
1896-1900

News of gold discovery in the Klondike galvanized Seattle where hundreds of would-be prospectors crowded every available ship north during the summer of 1898. (University of Alaska)

Gold Fever 1896–1900

For sheer frenzy, no gold rush in history could match the Klondike. Discovery of the yellow metal in the wilderness of northwestern Canada set off a stampede that drew fortune hunters from every corner of the world. Many braved incredible hardships in the all-too-often illusory hope of striking it rich.

Like ripples in a pond, the shock waves of gold discovery in the Klondike made a major city of Seattle, inaugurated large-scale steam navigation on the Yukon River as a vital transportation artery and, in a large measure, led to the settle-ment of the Yukon Territory and the interior of Alaska.

Discovery on the Klondike

In the summer of 1896, three men were work-ing along Rabbit Creek, a small tributary of the Klondike River. George Carmack, a white "squaw man" married to an Indian, and his two Indian companions, Skookum Jim and Tagish Charlie, had been fishing for salmon that sum-mer. The fishing was poor and they'd turned to cutting timber which they intended to float downriver to Forty Mile. Bending down to scoop drinking water from the stream, Skookum Jim discovered gold flakes scattered in the sand along the bottom.

By gentlemen's agreement, prospectors who made a strike were obliged to pass on the news of the discovery to other prospectors. After staking seven 500-foot claims along the banks of Rabbit Creek (soon to be renamed Bonanza), Carmack and Charlie boarded a log raft for Forty Mile, leaving Skookum Jim to guard their find.

Filing claims and announcing their discovery at Forty Mile, they galvanized the miners who promptly headed upstream as fast as they could go. Within days, the town was all but deserted.

By mid-September, prospectors had staked every inch of Bonanza Creek as well as its smaller tributaries and were taking out gold that ran $25 to $50 per pan and occasionally as high as $500 per pan.

With the onset of winter, difficult living conditions became nearly impossible, but the lure of gold drove them onward. Subsisting on flour, beans and sometimes smoked salmon, many of them contracted scurvy. They were sickly and ridden with lice. Home was a hastily constructed hut, lean-to or tent, filled with smoke and icy cold. Burrowing into the frozen ground, miners built fires to thaw the gold-bearing gravel, then piled it in dumps to be panned out in the spring. But the hardships paid off for some of these first Klondikers. They struck it rich beyond their wildest dreams. The average claim that winter produced about $600,000 and several topped the $1 million mark.

The Rush is On

Through the winter of 1896-97, only the few hundred prospectors already in the Yukon had any idea of the riches that had been discovered on Bonanza Creek. It took nearly a year from the discovery in August for the word to reach the outside world. But with the spring breakup two sternwheelers, ACC's *Alice* and NAT&T's *Portus B. Weare* arrived at nearby Dawson after the long journey upriver from St. Michael. When they departed they carried aboard several dozen miners, a ton and a half of gold and news of the Klondike strike.

On reaching St. Michael, passengers and their gold boarded the *Excelsior* bound for San Francisco and the *Portland* bound for Seattle. On July

Klondikers used every conceivable means to reach the goldfields. Here in September 1899, the sternwheeler A. J. Goddard *tows five rafts loaded with men and supplies. (Yukon Archives)*

43

15 the *Excelsior* touched off news of the strike in San Francisco and a day later the *Portland* landed a ton of gold in Seattle. The news flashed around the world. The Seattle Post-Intelligencer of July 17 carried the banner headlines:

GOLD! GOLD! GOLD! GOLD!

Sixty-Eight Rich Men on the Steamer Portland

STACKS OF YELLOW METAL!

Some have $5,000, Many Have More, and a Few Bring Out $100,000 Each.

THE STEAMER CARRIES $700,000

Within days thousands were scrambling for passage on any vessel headed north. During 1897 and 1898 more than 100,000 stampeded to the Yukon.

But getting there was no easy matter. Thousands of miles of stormy seas, rugged mountain passes, vast wilderness and a climate harsher than most could ever imagine faced these soldiers of fortune.

Up and Over the Pass

In 1897 only two practical routes to the Klondike existed. The first, via St. Michael, was by far the easiest, but it was also the longest. Passengers embarked on steamers at San Francisco, Portland, Vancouver, Victoria or Seattle to make the long sea voyage to the mouth of the Yukon. Seas were often stormy and many a craft, hastily pressed into service, was totally unfit for deep water steaming.

Once he arrived at "St. Mike", the would-be prospector boarded a sternwheeler that would take him up to Dawson, a trip usually requiring three to five weeks. If he started late in the season, he faced the prospect of being stuck at St. Michael by the freeze-up and his journey for riches might occupy nearly a year, by which time all the good prospects would, of course, be gone.

The routes over White or Chilcoot Passes were shorter and less expensive but had the stam-

Trading company warehouses stocked mountains of supplies to support the miners. This Northern Commercial Company warehouse at Dawson contains crates of candles, condensed milk, canned goods and mining tools. (University of Alaska)

On Yukon River '98 - Dawson or Bust

This primitive scow, beached at Dawson in 1898, has a boiler and steam engine that were probably lugged over Chilcoot Pass for construction on Lake Bennett. (University of Alaska)

peders known how rugged they would be, many of them would never have started out.

Steamers took them north to Dyea or Skagway, two boom camps at the head of fjord-like Lynn Canal. From here they had a choice of crossing White Pass or Chilcoot Pass to the headwaters of the Yukon River. The White Pass trail led some 45 miles over the mountains from Skagway to Lake Bennett; the Chilcoot covered 27 miles from Dyea to Lake Lindeman. Roughly parallel, the trails were about six miles apart, but pack animals could negotiate the easier White Pass route whereas they could not over Chilcoot.

More chose Chilcoot because it was shorter, it was open all year and, in the summer, it avoided the rotting carcasses of more than 3,000 pack animals that had died climbing White Pass. But no matter how short, it took the average stampeder about three months to pack his gear over the trail. The legendary Sam Steele and his North West Mounted Police stationed at the summit required each prospector entering British Columbia to have 1,150 pounds of food plus other essentials. Packing an average load of 70 pounds per man, the stampeders made many round trips to the summit. Indians hired out as packers and by May of 1898 a tram that could carry loads up to 400 pounds was operating over the last steep climb.

In winter the conditions were abominable. Thousands trudged up the "Golden Stairs", 1,200 steps cut in the ice of a near-vertical wall, to reach an elevation of 3,739 feet at the top. Blizzards raged across the pass and if the stampeder didn't freeze to death, he might be buried in one of the avalanches that periodically thundered down.

Once they reached the shores of Lake Bennett, the stampeders still had more than 500 miles to go to reach the goldfields. All winter long they camped in a tent city sprawled along the lakeshore and painstakingly whipsawed lumber into boats for the downstream voyage. They built all manner of craft—rafts, rowboats, scows, prams and dories—anything that would float. The lake was ice-free on May 29, 1898, and the following day more than 30,000 would-be prospectors with some 30 million pounds of gear in 7,124 boats headed for Dawson.

Among this unlikely flotilla were several small sternwheelers. Boilers and fittings for their construction had been hauled by man and animal over the passes. The *Bellingham* was the first to head downriver leaving Lake Bennett on June 5. Eight others followed and all but one successfully negotiated the treacherous white water of Miles Canyon, Whitehorse and Squaw Rapids. One casualty, the *Joseph Clossett*, smashed into the sheer canyon walls and sank at the head of the rapids.

This stretch of river was so dangerous the Mounted Police soon stepped in to require

Sternwheelers Australian, Gleaner *and* Nora *unloading miners and supplies at the head of Miles Canyon in 1899. From here the tramway will carry them around the rapids. (University of Washington)*

women and children walk the five miles around canyon and rapids, even if their foolhardy male companions wished to risk their lives in the attempt to run the river. By the summer of 1898 a wooden tramway had been constructed around the rapids and the prudent among the stampeders had their boats and outfits hauled overland for $25.

The Long Way Around

Meanwhile, at the other end of the Yukon, additional thousands were arriving on every available ship. But the demand for transportation upriver from St. Michael in 1897 exceeded the supply. In addition to the *Alice, P.B. Weare* and

St. Michael, there were the *Bella, John J. Healy, Northern Light, W. K. Merwin, S. B. Matthews, Milwaukee* and *May West,* far too few to carry the hordes bound for the Klondike.

Back in Seattle and San Francisco, unscrupulous operators were selling tickets for through transportation to Dawson that included passage on riverboats that didn't exist. The mayor of Seattle, W. D. Wood, formed one such company whose passengers arrived in St. Michael to find themselves stranded. Not letting that small difficulty stand in their way, they turned to and helped build *Seattle No. 1.* Unfortunately, the job wasn't finished until so late in the season they were caught in the freeze-up and didn't reach

Dawson until the following June. Thousands of stampeders were stranded at St. Michael and along the Yukon during the winter of 1897-98. Many of them were destitute, not having brought enough supplies to last more than the few weeks they anticipated it would take to reach the Klondike.

A long-standing policy of the Alaska Commercial Company saved many of them. Set down by President Lewis Gerstle in 1886, instructions to company traders read in part: "... in case of absolute poverty or want, the person or persons placed in that unfortunate position should be promptly furnished with the means of subsistence without pay, simply reporting such facts at your earliest convenience to the home office."

Food supplies that winter were short all along the river. On the last upriver trip of the 1897 season the *Bella* and *P. B. Weare* were stranded by low water in the Yukon Flats. Unloading part of their cargos, they managed to work their way over the sandbars and arrived in Circle City to be confronted by angry miners. Food stocks were low and the miners, at gunpoint, demanded 57 tons of supplies that were destined for Dawson, be unloaded on the spot.

When the two vessels arrived in Dawson, short of the needed cargo, Inspector C. Constantine of the NWMP posted a prophetic notice that read: "... having carefully looked over the present distressing situation in regard to the supply of food for the winter, [government officials] find that the stock on hand is not sufficient ... For those who have not laid in a winter's supply to remain here longer is to court death from starvation ... Starvation now stares everyone in the face who is hoping and waiting for outside relief."

Hundreds jammed the decks of the steamboats headed downriver.

Robert Service, the bard of the Klondike, made the terrors of a Yukon winter familiar to readers all over the world with his stanzas of "The Cremation of Sam McGee." The poem is taken from a real incident that occurred when a winter patrol of the NWMP discovered a prospector

A.C. Cove at St. Michael around the turn of the century was boatyard and winter quarters for many sternwheelers that plied the Yukon. (Yukon Archives)

Officers and crew of the S.S. Bailey *posed for a portrait in August of 1899. Uniform coats and caps were the order of the day on this sternwheeler. (Yukon Archives)*

dying of scurvy in a cabin on "the marge of Lake Leberge. [sic]" A doctor was summoned but arrived too late. Unable to bury the body in the frozen ground, he cremated it in the firebox of the *Olive May,* a steamer that had been frozen into the lake for the winter.

A Trio of Floating Palaces

A frantic shipbuilding program took place that winter on the beaches of St. Michael, in San Francisco, Puget Sound and at Alaska ports such as Dutch Harbor.

The Moran shipyard in Seattle turned out an even dozen, "building them by the mile and cutting them off when necessary." The Canadian Pacific Railway was in the process of building 20 vessels for the Stikine River when the rush began and immediately transferred several of them to the Yukon. Others were "kit built", constructed at West Coast ports and shipped in pieces to be reassembled in St. Michael.

The demand for riverboats was so great, boilers and engines were taken from wrecked boats and installed in new hulls. By the spring of 1898, 30 new navigation companies had been formed to compete with ACC and NAT&T. More than 60 new boats and barges had been built to navigate the Yukon.

Alaska Exploration Company, Seattle-Yukon Transportation Company and Empire Transportation Company were the leaders among the newcomers. Other companies were formed on very shaky financial bases; many of them went broke before they ever operated a vessel. At least one solicited advance payments for passenger and freight tickets and attempted to build the steamer on the proceeds. Others formed a co-operative system, whereby a passenger could pay for his ticket by working for the company.

During the summer of 1898 ACC introduced three new steamboats that revolutionized the quality of Yukon transportation. The *Susie*, *Sarah* and *Hannah* were virtual floating palaces by comparison to the rude accommodations of previous riverboats. Built in Unalaska and towed to St. Michael, the three were named for the wives of company officials: the *Susie* for Mrs. Gustav Niebaum, the *Sarah* for Mrs. Louis Sloss and the *Hannah* for Mrs. Lewis Gerstle. All were 1,130-ton boats, 222 feet long by 42 feet in the beam, mounting engines of 1,000 horsepower that could drive them at 17 knots in slack water.

Designed after Mississippi River packetboats, the three were lavish in appointments. Two and three-berth staterooms slept 225 passengers including the "blue room", an elegant accommodation for distinguised guests located on the Texas deck. Staterooms were supplied with fresh linen and running water, a novelty among the riverboats whose passengers were usually required to draw water from the river by means of bucket and rope.

Uniformed stewards served meals in a spacious dining room trimmed in mahogany and furnished with heavy plate silver service monogrammed with the company's initials. Just forward of the dining salon, the observation lounge, furnished with thick rugs and plush upholstered furniture, provided a comfortable place to relax with unobstructed views of the river through wraparound forward windows. Thrashing their way up the river at night, ablaze with lights, these new steamers brought a festive air to the Yukon.

Though the all-water route to the Klondike was considered the most expensive of the two alternatives, the fares seem ridiculously low by modern standards. A first-class passenger ticket from San Francisco to St. Michael cost $120. An additional $90 was charged on the upriver trip to Dawson. The downstream rate of $65 was less because the trip took less time.

The *Susie* was the first to arrive at the gold-fields on August 9, 1898 followed by the *Hannah* on September 1 and the *Sarah* on September 22.

Boom Towns

Sleepy little St. Michael was overrun in the summer of '98. More than 20,000 people passed through between June and September. The town was a frenzy of activity with new hotels, warehouses, stores and saloons springing up almost daily. A dozen or more steamboats under construction shared the muddy beach with hundreds of tent dwellers.

With the boom came the inevitable crime. In St. Michael, and at other points along the river, murder, robbery and assault were common. Gamblers and bunco artists traveled the riverboats, lying in wait for the greenhorns.

Unlike the Canadian end of the river that was well policed by the North West Mounted Police, Alaska had no law enforcement. The responsibility fell to the Army.

Destitute miners causing trouble at St. Michael prompted NAT & T to call for the troops.

In 1897 Lt. Colonel George M. Randall with four commissioned officers and 218 enlisted men of the 8th Infantry, under the Department of the Columbia headquartered at Vancouver Barracks, Washington, founded Fort St. Michael. A detachment of Battery D, 3rd Artillery, with one officer and 74 enlisted men followed in 1898. By the summer of 1899 they were augmented by two companies of the 7th Infantry who constructed and garrisoned a new post at Fort Gibbon (now Tanana) midway upriver. Another garrison was established at Eagle City the same year.

Dawson, meanwhile, had exploded from Joseph Ladue's sawmill, warehouse and cabin-cum-saloon in 1896 to a rowdy young city of more than 25,000 by the summer of 1898. Dawson and its neighbor across the river, Louse-town, boasted banks, newspapers, theaters, churches, a telephone service, dozens of retail businesses, saloons, dance halls, brothels and an NWMP detachment of nearly 300.

Prices fluctuated from astonomical to rock bottom depending on the amount of supplies delivered by the constant parade of riverboats. In the summer of 1898 the Klondiker would typically pay $1.30 for an orange or lemon, $25 for a watermelon, $20 to $40 a pint for champagne to celebrate his strike or drown his disappointment. As with other gold rush towns throughout the history of the West, many who made fortunes were not miners but merchants.

Of the thousands who made the arduous trek to the Klondike, only a handful were rewarded for their effort. They arrived to find all of the producing creeks long since claimed. In fact, virtually all of the rich ground had been staked before they even began their journey. Many stayed in Dawson only a few days, then headed downriver in their homemade boats or caught a steamer for St. Michael. Others lingered, rushing off to remote sites at the slightest hint of a strike, hoping against hope that this would be the big one.

Ironically, the Klondike Gold Rush was over almost before it began. Discovered in 1896, booming in the next three years, it had virtually petered out by the turn of the century. By 1899 the big, well-financed mining companies were moving in to buy out individual claims and set up hydraulic mining and dredging with expensive apparatus that would continue until 1966.

Discovery of gold on the beaches of Nome in July 1899 brought an end to the Klondike Rush. Hearing of the new strike, thousands of miners jammed every available boat going downriver to St. Michael and within weeks Dawson, although not deserted, saw its days of glory fade. Though the region's peak production of $22 million annually was not reached until 1900, more than half of Dawson's inhabitants were already gone.

The Coming of the Railroad

If the Klondike Gold Rush was the single factor most responsible for making Yukon navigation into a full-fledged industry, the completion of the White Pass and Yukon Railway was to have even greater effects in insuring the longevity of the steamboats on the upper river. At the same time, it hastened the demise of St. Michael on the lower river.

Begun at Skagway in May 1898, the narrow-gauge line was pushed 110 miles over White Pass to Lake Bennett by July 1900. Gone were the difficult hauls by man and animal over White and Chilcoot Passes. Passengers and freight could now reach Dawson from Seattle in eight days via the railroad and connecting steamers. Heavy cargo that once had to travel the long and expensive route via St. Michael could now move over the railroad in less time and at less cost. Soon to follow, a new fleet of sternwheelers would dominate the upper Yukon for more than half a century.

V

THE RIVERBOATS COME OF AGE
1900-1916

Chena (Fairbanks) waterfront about 1905. The Julia B *was a Merchant's Yukon Line sternwheeler of 835 tons, built at Ballard, Washington. (University of Alaska)*

THE RIVERBOATS COME OF AGE 1900-1916

The opening years of the 20th century saw tremendous change in Yukon River navigation. The gold rush was petering out and, although there would be others, none would generate the river commerce the Klondike had.

Commerce along the Yukon was maturing. Whereas, prior to 1900, dozens of riverboats were primarily occupied with carrying freight and passengers to the goldfields, now trading posts were scattered in villages all along the river. Freight was just as often groceries, building materials and trade goods as it was gold and furs. And, the boats were helping to develop trade along the side streams as well. Sternwheelers made regular runs up the Pelly, Stewart, Porcupine, Tanana, Koyukuk, Iditarod and Innoko, calling at isolated villages, mining camps and trading posts.

A whole collection of small companies and independent operators ran dozens of steamboats carrying passengers and cargo to any destination that had sufficient water to float a boat. Some eked out a bare living; others lasted only a season or two, then sold their boats or left them beached and rotting.

By 1901 even the big operators, Alaska Commercial and North American Transportation and Trading, were finding it difficult to make a profit.

In April of that year ACC merged with Alaska Exploration Company and Empire Transportation Company to form Northern Navigation Company. From now on NCC would operate the river steamers and a related firm, Northern Commercial Company, would operate the trading posts.

The *Arnold, Linda, Leon, Mary F. Graff* and *F. K. Gustin,* formerly owned by AEC, were added to the new fleet. All were between 690 and 870 tons and had been built at Dutch Harbor and Seattle in 1898. Empire Transportation contributed the *Empire, Alaska (I), Seattle* No. 2 and *Tacoma.* The *Empire* was one of the real curiosities on the river with a steel hull and driven by six propellers. Appropriately, rivermen nicknamed her, "The Six Shooter."

A New Strike at Fairbanks

In July 1901 the *Lavelle Young,* a sternwheeler built in Portland three years previously, thrashed her way up the shallow Tanana River. Aboard was Captain E. T. Barnette with 125 tons of trade goods who had come from Circle City with the intention of setting himself up in business with the Indians. About 400 miles upstream the *Lavelle Young* encountered water too shallow to proceed further and the captain, his wife and trade goods were unceremoniously dumped ashore. They found themselves stranded on the banks of the Chena River, a tributary of the Tanana.

Though it wasn't where he intended to stop and there wasn't an Indian in sight, the circumstances were fortunate for Barnette. His first

Steamboat racing was a favorite pastime of Yukon skippers. Here the Bailey *races an unidentified vessel along the Fifty Mile River in 1899.*

53

customer was Felix Pedro, an Italian immigrant who had been prospecting creeks in the area. Barnette erected a trading post that fall and, a year later, was among the first to learn of Pedro's gold strike on nearby Discovery Creek.

Barnette made his fortune on the thousands of miners who flooded in in the following months. The strike proved to be the richest in Alaska's history, eventually yielding $35 million and making Fairbanks the largest city in Alaska by 1910. (Alaska's population reached a peak in 1910 that would not be equaled again until World War II.)

Riverboats played a major role in the development of the fledgling community. Mining methods had matured by the time of the Fairbanks strike. The gold was buried deep in frozen ground and mining companies brought in hydraulic monitors and at least seven dredges to process gravel on a large scale. All this heavy equipment meant cargo for the riverboats over the next decade and a half.

The busy waterfront on Chena Slough soon saw flotillas of sternwheelers coming and going each season. The Tanana Valley Railroad (a narrow-gauge line) was built to connect the towns of Chena and Fairbanks with the goldfields. Navigation companies altered their routes up and down the Yukon to include a trip up the Tanana to Chena and Fairbanks and established the village of Tanana (on the Yukon) as a transfer point between boats plying the upper and lower rivers and the side streams.

White Pass & Yukon Takes to the Water

That same year, 1901, saw another major competitor move into river commerce. The White Pass & Yukon Railway purchased the fleet of John Irving Navigation Company and the winter stage line operated by the Canadian Development Company beween Whitehorse and Dawson. In a single move, the British-owned railroad company had become the most important navigation firm on the upper Yukon as well as on the headwaters lakes, including Atlin and Bennett.

Operating under the name of British Yukon Navigation (BYN), the White Pass built a large shipyard, warehouses and vessel storage facilities at Whitehorse. From Canadian Development they inherited the *Canadian, Columbian, Sybil* and *Yukoner,* all under 800 tons and built in Victoria in 1898.

Accelerated construction on the ways at Whitehorse produced three new vessels, the *Dawson* (779 tons), the *Selkirk* (777 tons) and the pride of the fleet, the 1,120-ton *White Horse.* The *Selkirk* soon established the speed record from Dawson to Whitehorse of two days, 17 hours. The *White Horse,* nicknamed "The Old Gray Mare", was completed in just 43 days from the laying of her keel.

The Yukon Design

Though a few propeller driven boats and at least one sidewheeler saw service on the Yukon,

Winter quarters in Whitehorse in 1901 with the British Yukon Navigation Co. fleet up on the ways. Boats include the White Horse *and* Victorian. *(Yukon Archives)*

The Suzie *was one of three "floating palaces" built by Alaska Commercial Company at Dutch Harbor in 1898 for service between St. Michael and Dawson. (University of Alaska)*

the vast majority were steam-driven stern-wheelers. Sidewheelers, so popular on the eastern rivers, could not respond to steering fast enough, got hung up in the brush and trees overhanging the Yukon's banks and needed a pier or other fixed landing place to discharge cargo.

The first sternwheelers, constructed at West Coast ports, at Dutch Harbor and at St. Michael, followed traditional Mississippi and Ohio River designs. Many of them quickly proved unsuitable for the fast moving water and narrow channels of the Yukon. New designs for very shallow draft vessels with tremendous backing power evolved.

Typically, the Yukon steamer was flat bottomed, drawing no more than four feet of water fully loaded. Steam produced by a large boiler on the freight deck powered piston engines which, in turn, moved large Pitman arms synchronized to turn the paddlewheels. Wooden bladed paddlewheels were huge, often 20 feet high and more than 20 feet across, and could provide thrust drawing as little as six inches of water.

Wood was the principal fuel. But, in 1903, NNC and NAT&T converted several of the larger boats that ran through the treeless delta to oil. Four 5,000 gallon supply tanks were built at St. Michael with additional tanks at Andreafski, Kaltag, Tanana and Circle. The steamers that burned wood purchased it for about $7 a cord at the turn-of-the-century and burned between one

and three cords an hour when beating their way upstream.

The superstructure of these boats varied according to the size of the boat, the resources of the company that built it and its principal use. Some simple cargo boats resembled a box on a raft; others, the elegant passenger vessels, were complete with wooden "gingerbread", mahogany railings and fancy fretwork.

The bottom or freight deck was usually occupied by cordwood stacked in every available inch of space around the boiler and engine; on some vessels the crew's quarters were also on this deck. The next deck above the waterline commonly covered most of the boat's length (125 feet on the average) and most of its beam (typically, 30-plus feet). Known as the passenger or saloon deck, it contained staterooms, dining room, gallery and lounges on passenger steamers, crew's quarters and a few spartan cabins on boats devoted primarily to freight. Officers' cabins and the most elegant passenger cabins occupied the Texas deck, usually a narrow deckhouse running only about half the length of the passenger deck beneath it. Perched atop the superstructure, the pilot house commanded superb views in all directions.

Some freight and mail were carried on the freight deck, but most sternwheelers pushed cargo-laden barges ahead of them. Four barges

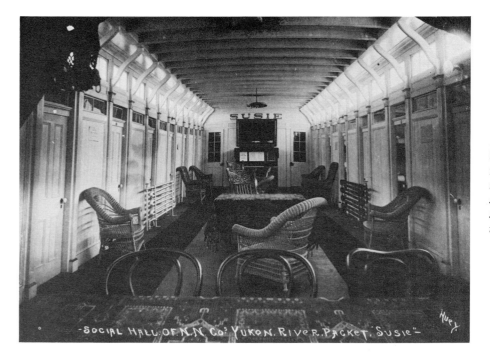

SOCIAL HALL OF N.N Co. YUKON. RIVER.PACKET. "SUSIE"

Passenger lounges on the Suzie *(here),* Sarah *and* Hannah *were comfortably furnished, served by uniformed stewards and included musical entertainment. (University of Alaska)*

lashed in pairs or in a tandem pyramid arrangement were common. NNC's *Louise,* one of the most powerful boats on the river, was said to be capable of pushing eight or nine loaded barges between St. Michael and Tanana.

Crews ranged from a dozen to twenty or more men. Firemen, deckhands and roustabouts were often Indians as were some pilots. At the turn-of-the century pilots, mates and pursers drew about $100 a month, engineers $120, cooks $50 to $75. Firemen and deckhands were paid about $2 per day. Captains earned an annual salary of about $2,500 that included board and lodging in company hotels during the winter months.

On the fanciest of the riverboats old-timers recall, "People dressed for dinner and the waiters all wore white jackets. There were pianos on the old boats and sometimes shows."

Describing a voyage on NNC's *Susie* in 1908, passenger Clara Hickman Rust wrote, "The dining room could be reached from the staterooms without going outside. We were called to meals by the sound of a small xylophone . . . The food was good, plentiful and well served . . . All of the woodwork was painted white with a little gold trim . . . There was a piano in the salon but nobody to play it. There was also a Victrola and we danced to its music . . . helped out by one of the men from Nome on his zither." All in all, the best of the boats provided rather festive atmosphere in the midst of a wilderness.

The Also Rans

Three big companies now accounted for most of the traffic on the river. In 1906 more than 32,000 tons of freight moved through St. Michael and up the river. Most of it was carried by Northern Navigation's 17 steamers and 25 barges or by North American Transportation's ten steamers and 11 barges. Independent operators ran three boats and four barges, not including several mail launches.

But the small companies managed to survive and even built a few new boats. In 1901 the Stewart River Co. built the 165-ton *Prospector.* Cy Atwell operated the 71-ton Fairbanks-built *Little Delta* on the Iditarod in 1908. Merchant's Yukon Line built the 835-ton *Julia B* at Ballard the same year.

Frequently they existed on the leavings after the big companies had skimmed off the most lucrative trade. The independents faced other problems as well. Harry Young, first officer of NNC's *Louise* in 1906, remarked, "Sometimes the steamer gets hung up [on a sandbar] for several days. The independent steamers are at a disadvantage as one of our [NNC's] boats will pass and help us off; but the independent fellow has to get off the best he can, or pay for a line."

With a need to supply Forts Gibbon and Egbert as well as the relay stations of the Washington-Alaska Military Cable and Telegraph at Nenana,

The little 28-ton North Star frozen in on a slough on the upper river. The boat was built at St. Michael in 1898 and is typical of those operated by the small independent companies. (Anchorage Historical and Fine Arts Museum)

Fire aboard the Yukoner *at Dawson on May 2, 1900. The blaze was apparently non-fatal for she was operated by British Yukon Navigation until 1903 and ended her days as a lumber storage facility in Whitehorse. (Yukon Archives)*

Steamers Tanana *and* Dusty Diamond *land stampeders on Iditerod River beach in 1910. Several small gold rushes on the side streams followed the Klondike. (University of Alaska)*

Company G, 10th U.S. Infantry, on parade at Fort St. Michael about 1906. Troops were brought into Alaska to provide law and order on the frontier. (Anchorage Historical and Fine Arts Museum)

Minto, Birches, Koyukuk, Kaltag, Old Woman, Rampart, Hogan and Delta, the Army brought two sternwheelers to the river in the early part of the century. The *General Jefferson C. Davis* had been built at Port Blakely, Washington, as the *Duchesnay* and used for awhile at Cook's Inlet before being brought to St. Michael. The *General J. W. Jacobs* was built for the Army at Whitehorse in 1908 at a cost of $30,000. The Quartermaster Corps operated them without any fixed schedule, but as the needs of the service dictated. Until 1910 they were based at St. Michael, but moved to Fort Gibbon with the completion of new marine facilities that year.

Whether these two boats were cheaply constructed or just poorly maintained is not known, but judging by available records neither was very efficient. Though both were frequently laid up for repairs, they did manage to survive into the mid-1930s.

In 1906 North American Trading and Transportation gave up the ghost, selling all of its fleet and marine facilities at St. Michael to Merchants' Yukon Transportation Company. Just three years later, the White Pass expanded by forming the Side Stream Navigation Company to run boats on the White, Stewart, Pelly and Porcupine Rivers. They operated the shallow draft 134-ton *Vidette* (former *May West*), 145-ton *Pauline* and the 405-ton *Nasutlin* (known to rivermen as the "Nasty").

S.S. Bailey, *first steamer of the season to arrive in Dawson, May 23, 1901. The whole town turned out for the event which signaled the arrival of fresh groceries. (University of Alaska)*

Side Stream Navigation Co. steamer Vidette *on her way up the White River in 1913 to put miners ashore two days' walk from new diggings. (University of Alaska)*

Bennett Lake and Klondike Navigation Company's Flora *at a wood stop on the upper Yukon. Note well-dressed woman passenger and small boy in cap and knickers. (University of Alaska)*

Steamer Rock Island *frozen-in for winter at slough near Dawson. Burned hulk is* Glendora *or* Mona *after both were destroyed by fire March 27, 1902. (Yukon Archives)*

Wrecks and Other Disasters

At one period it seemed there were more steamboats being lost to accident than were being built. The *Jeff Davis* collided with NAT&T's *Mary Ann* in 1900, the same year that the *Florence S* capsized in the Thirty Mile River drowning three and the *Gold Star* was wrecked in Five Finger Rapids. Another Army vessel, the *Katie Hemrich*, sank at Nulato. The *La France* wrecked herself on the Thirty Mile in 1911, the *Leah* at Kaltag. One boat, the *Phillip B. Low*, sank so many times she was nicknamed, "The Fillup Below."

Some boats (or at least parts of them) seemed to have nine lives, being resurrected again and again. In 1902 NNC built the first *Koyukuk* for work on the river of the same name. She was wrecked on the Tanana in 1904. Two years later her machinery was installed in the second *Koyukuk,* a 254-ton sternwheeler. She managed to serve the Koyukuk River and St. Michael-Fairbanks runs for four more years until lost on the Chena. Undaunted, the company salvaged the same machinery and installed it in a new hull they christened *M. L. Washburn* (after NNC's general manager and nicknamed "Shaggy Dog"). The *Washburn* survived until 1920 when she was wrecked at the mouth of the Stewart River.

Northern Navigation's *City of Paris* suffered an unusual fate. Frozen in on the Koyukuk River in the winter of 1901-02, she was rumored to have a large cargo of liquor aboard. Locals searching for a little internal warmth generated a

Ill-fated Columbian *departs on her last voyage down the Yukon from Whitehorse in September 1906. The British Yukon Navigation Co. vessel was built in Victoria in 1898. (Yukon Archives)*

lot more heat than they intended. They accidentally set her on fire and she burned to the waterline. Ironically, the liquor had already been removed and was stored in a warehouse ashore.

Perhaps the most bizarre accident to befall a Yukon riverboat struck the *Columbian* in 1906. The BYN sternwheeler was making her way from Whitehorse to Dawson on the last trip of the season. Among the cargo were three tons of explosives stored on the freight deck. It was common practice in those days for crew members to shoot waterfowl or moose from the decks of a passing steamer. On this occasion the would-be hunter stumbled and fired into the powder. The resulting explosion killed six and set the boat afire, destroying it.

St. Michael, Norton Sound and the mouth of the Yukon claimed many victims over the years.

Shallow water forced ocean-going freighters to anchor two or three miles offshore and lighter cargo at St. Michael. Frequent storms forced them to interrupt unloading and seek shelter behind one of the islands to the north or run for the safety of the open sea. On the run to the Apoon mouth of the Yukon, the frail river sternwheelers were exposed to the battering waves of Norton Sound before they could enter one of the delta waterways. For the next 42 miles, the water was so shallow and so subject to wind and tides that strandings were common.

It's questionable whether any solution would have been found had not the Army begun to operate its own sternwheelers through the same treacherous channels by 1900. In 1908 the Army Engineers began straightening and deepening St. Michael Canal, a six-mile, hundred-foot wide

The James Domville *struck the rocks and sank in the Thirty Mile River in the spring of 1899, less than a year after her launching at North Vancouver.* (Yukon Archives)

All that's left of the Columbian *after a careless crewman fired a gun into her cargo of explosives. Passengers had to hike the long miles to Dawson. (Yukon Archives)*

Steamers. Next day after Hauling out.
Taken Oct 11 1907. J.R.IU.

Northern Navigation Company sternwheelers wintered at Fairbanks in 1907. Shown are the Tanana,
Reliance, Koyukuk *and* Delta. *(University of Alaska)*

shortcut behind St. Michael Island. Working with an 18-inch hydraulic dredge and $507,000 in Federal funds, they completed the project and dredged the mouth of the Yukon by 1915. It is virtually the only instance when the government provided any navigation assistance to the Yukon riverboats and, when it came, it came too late to be of much use.

A Shift in the Balance of Power

By 1911 the balance of traffic along the Yukon had clearly shifted. Though the amount of freight shipped through St. Michael reached an all-time high of 33,669 tons that year, 94% of it was destined for American customers with a mere 2,135 tons trickling into Canadian waters. Traf-

fic over the White Pass & Yukon Railway and down the upper Yukon was still healthy, but Dawson was declining. It was time for the Canadians to make a move.

Within two years the White Pass formed another river subsidiary, the American Yukon Navigation Co. (AYN). With two brand new steamboats, the *Alaska* and the *Yukon*, built at Whitehorse in 1913, plus others borrowed from British Yukon Navigation, the company began intense competition between Dawson and St. Michael.

Northern Navigation, now the only U.S. company of any size, retaliated by sending the *Norcom* into Canadian territory to operate between Dawson and Whitehorse. Within weeks the two

American Yukon Navigation Co.'s Yukon *is docked at Nenana and unloading men and mules for the surveying parties laying out the Alaska Railroad. (University of Alaska)*

rivals engaged in a ruinous rate war that saw fares from Whitehorse to Dawson decline from $26 to $5. The White Pass, in turn, cut through freight rates from Seattle to Chena from $45 to $25 per ton. If the hostilities continued, both companies would soon be bankrupt.

In the spring of 1914, Northern Navigation agreed to sell out to AYN and leave the Cana-

Fairbanks citizens welcome home Judge Wickersham, August 23, 1908. The Reliance and the Schwatka were both Northern Navigation Company vessels. (University of Alaska)

dians in charge of the river. With the sale went 42 steamboats, 54 barges and all marine facilities on the entire Yukon system, including the side-streams. White Pass had won the day, but their triumph was to be short lived.

An Independent Founds an Empire

The pages of Yukon River history are replete with larger-than-life characters. Men who explored its wilderness, men who ran its lonely trading posts, men who commanded its steamboats—all have made their mark.

George Black was such a man.

Black might have been a mere footnote, a small-time riverman who plied the side streams for a few years, then faded and was gone. He might have been, except for one thing. In 1916 George Black founded a navigation company that was to operate longer than any other and would emerge as the sole survivor of Yukon River transportation.

Born in Ballard, Washington, Black moved north to Cordova at an early age, where his father operated deep water boats. By the time he had reached manhood, he'd drifted to Skagway, then across the mountains to Whitehorse and a job as steward on the sternwheelers run by the White Pass companies.

Art Peterson, Black's son-in-law and founder of Yutana Barge Lines, remembers him as one of a tough breed of rivermen. "His nickname was 'Stormy' because of the way he dealt with knotty problems," says Peterson. "Two incidents say a lot about George. When he was in Skagway, he was working in a sawmill. One day, he slipped and fell into the saw, opening up his chest from one end to the other. Well, he walked into the hospital, dripping blood and all, casual as you please. It took more than 140 stitches to close the wound.

"When he decided to get a job on the Yukon riverboats, he was flat broke and couldn't afford the rail fare from Skagway to Whitehorse. So, he set out walking and hoofed it all the way to Whitehorse for a job."

In 1916 Black, now in his early 20s, with one small steamboat, the *Pioneer*, started a navigation company to serve the side streams where isolated mining camps were too small for the attentions of the big AYN boats.

Like many of the small operators at that time, Black became a jack-of-all-trades in order to survive. In addition to hauling groceries, dry goods, machinery, dried fish, ore and furs, he acted as a floating peddler, trading anything off the *Pioneer* the miners needed. During the winter he turned to woodcutting around Fairbanks, both to supply fuel for the boat for the following season and to sell to local customers.

It was a tough way to make a living but Black would hang on for nearly 40 years. His company and his heirs would outlast everyone else on the river.

VI

THE COMING OF THE RAILROAD
1916-1940

The Tanana, *built at St. Michael in 1904 by Northern Navigation Co. and operated by American Yukon Navigation, calls at Eagle, first stop in the U.S. after leaving Canada. (University of Alaska)*

The Coming of the Railroad
1916–1940

Ever since Fairbanks had become a town, Alaskans living in the interior had been pressing the territorial government for a better system of transportation. The navigation companies did the job from either end of the Yukon during the summer months, but inhabitants were virtually cut off the rest of the year.

In 1905 the Nelson Act established the Alaska Road Commission to begin construction of roads to the interior. By 1930 the commission had constructed nearly 5,000 miles of roads and trails, the most important of which was the Richardson Road connecting Valdez and Fairbanks.

In the meantime, railroad entrepreneurs made several abortive attempts to connect the interior and the coast with steel. The Alaska Northern Railroad actually completed 71 miles of track toward Fairbanks before it went bankrupt.

Taking over from these beginnings in 1915 the Alaska Railroad, a federally run company operated by the Department of the Interior, began pushing the rails northward to connect Seward, on salt water, with Fairbanks. Anchorage, now Alaska's largest city, began as a railroad construction camp supplying the nearly 5,000 men (many of them Indians) who pushed the rails slowly but inexorably past Mt. McKinley, the coalfields at Healy and the Tanana River.

The Railroad Takes to the River

Anyone with a map of Alaska could see the

railroad would deal a mortal blow to the White Pass & Yukon's rail-river monopoly on the Yukon. In 1922 the WP & Y subsidiary, American Yukon Navigation, retaliated, withdrawing all riverboat service from the Tanana (and Fairbanks). They continued to operate sporadic service that summer on the Yukon itself with the *Alaska* and *Yukon*. Several small local boats (including George Black's *Pioneer*) were hastily pressed into service to handle the Tanana and Chena traffic, but they weren't enough. The Army had to use the *General J. W. Jacobs* to pick up stranded miners and trappers all along the river during the summer.

With the completion of the rails to Nenana, the Alaska Railroad established its River Boat Service in 1922. The Army had been phasing out the posts along the Yukon and having no further need for the decrepit *Davis* and *Jacobs* turned them over to the railroad that fall. On July 15, 1923, President Warren G. Harding drove the golden spike at the north end of the new bridge across the Tanana at Nenana, completing the Alaska Railroad.

The link was forged and it had a pronounced effect on the transportation system of interior Alaska. From now on, freight and passengers destined for Fairbanks could get there by rail. Traffic destined for the villages along the Yukon could be brought in by rail, transferred to boats and barges at Nenana and transshipped by water. St. Michael would die on the vine, with dozens of steamboats littering her beaches to rot.

The new route to Fairbanks from Seattle by steamer and rail saved 2,395 miles over the old all-water route. And, it could be used twelve months of the year.

Mindful of the ruinous rate war that had put the Northern Navigation Company out of business less than a decade before (and that they only had two boats with which to cover the river), the Alaska Railroad reached a "gentlemen's agreement" with American Yukon Navigation. The Canadian boats would handle the upper river from Dawson down to Tanana and steam up the Tanana River to the rail transfer point at Nenana. The railroad would take the lower river, operating from Nenana down the Tenana and Yukon as far as Holy Cross (later extended to Marshall). Northern Commercial Company operated several small gasoline launches and diesel tugs out of St. Michael, serving company stores in the delta area and ran a regular gas boat service of one boat per week as far upriver as Holy Cross to connect with the railroad's weekly steamer from Nenana.

The Lean Years

There has always been controversy over the role of the federal government in operating the Alaska Railroad versus private enterprise, but in the case of the River Boat Service, AAR performed a public service that probably would not have been undertaken by independent companies. At least private operators would not have served the needs of the Yukon villages as reliably.

George Black, founder of Black Navigation Co., a forerunner of Yutana Barge Lines, and his first boat, the sternwheeler Pioneer *at Nenana. (Arthur Peterson)*

69

The boats were constant money losers in the 1920s. In 1926 the service lost more than $22,000, increasing to a deficit of more than $27,000 in 1928. Freight tonnages were modest; 3,125 in 1925 to 3,826 in 1928. Passengers were scarce: 721 in 1927 and 892 in 1928, for example.

The Canadians had the same problems. After 1924, AYN operated only the *Yukon* on the run to Nenana. The *Alaska* was returned to BYN to operate in Canada and renamed *Aksala*.

In 1927 AYN sold four boats to the Alaska Railroad: *Alice*, *White Seal*, *Minneapolis* and *Reliance*. *Minneapolis* and *Reliance* were beached at Chena, *White Seal* was resold and the *Alice*, best of the lot, was immediately pressed into service to augment the two aging ex-Army steamers.

Day Navigation Is Born

With only two boats in regular service, AAR had all it could do to serve the Tanana and Yukon Rivers. Customers on the side streams were served by Black Navigation and other small operators on a sporadic basis. By 1927 mining had increased around Flat on the Iditarod River and the Riley Investment Company, desperate for supplies, underwrote a new riverboat service that was destined to become another of the ancestors of Yutana Barge Lines.

Glenn Day had come to Flat as engineer on a gold dredge. With the company's backing, he and three partners founded Day Navigation Company. Rather than picking up any of the dozens of surplus river steamers now available, as other newcomers had done, they had two brand-new towboats designed especially for the extremely shallow waters they would encounter on the 410-mile run from Holy Cross up the Innoko and Iditarod Rivers to the village of Iditarod.

Built by the Lake Washington Shipyard at Houghton, Washington, *Danaco No. 1* and *Danaco No. 2*, plus two barges, were freighted north, assembled in Fairbanks and run down-

U.S. Army steamer General J. W. Jacobs *loading cargo at Nenana, September 4, 1922. Note the old covered wooden barge, typical on the Yukon before 1940. (Anchorage Historical and Fine Arts Museum)*

Log of the Alaska Railroad's General J. W. Jacobs *for September 1925. Entries for the 27th describe helping another Alaska RR steamer,* General Jefferson C. Davis, *at Ruby. (Anchorage Historical and Fine Arts Museum)*

stream to enter service. Both were tunnel boats and ideally suited to side stream work. Powered by a gas engine, *Danaco No. 2* was 65 feet long and drew just six inches of water! Slightly larger, *Danaco No. 1* was powered by twin 65-horsepower Atlas diesels and drew about 18 inches.

Tunnel boats were not new to the Yukon system, but their design adapted screw-driven vessels to operate efficiently in very shallow water. The shaft and screws of these vessels were recessed into "tunnels" in the stern that permitted water to flow over and be driven by the screw, but left no projecting blades beneath the hull to snag on sandbars and debris. All of the towboats now operating on the Yukon employ this design.

Day prospered and by 1930 had built a new 110-foot barge to make four trips a season to St. Michael, hauling back gasoline and groceries for the miners on the Iditarod. Northern Commercial had added a new 72-foot diesel tug, the *Encee*, to their fleet in 1927 for the St. Michael-Marshall run. George Turner and Ira Woods, who owned a store in Flat, also plied the Iditarod in these years with their small sternwheeler, *Nancy Belle*.

Wooding Up

Though an increasing number of boats on the Yukon were powered by gasoline or diesel engines, the three major companies—Alaska Railroad, American Yukon Navigation and British Yukon Navigation—still used woodburning, steam-powered sternwheelers.

Traders along the river contracted with the steamship companies to supply cordwood and stack it at designated stops along the bank. Natives cut most of the wood in the winter and were generally paid in trade goods by the contractor.

"Wooding up" was a tedious, back breaking job that steamboat men had to accomplish at least once a day going downriver, two or three times a day heading upstream. In his book, *Sternwheels on the Yukon*, probably the best existing account of steamboat life, Arthur E. Knutson describes the process.

"Short planks called double-enders were used to span the distance from the bow to shore. Then came another experience—building a portable road for the wood carts. We used five hand trucks at a time, one man to a truck. These trucks were nothing more than heavy duty longshore two-wheel trucks with angle cleats. A head board was installed in the blade end of the truck [to keep the wood from rolling off].

"These trucks were pulled behind us, loaded with about a third of a cord of wood. The deckhand would go down one side of the boat to the boiler where three deckhands were assigned to stowing. [On the next trip he] would go down the other side of the boiler to even up the load.

The Julia B *"wooding up" along the Yukon. All hands and often passengers turned to on this chore. These soldiers are probably from Fort Gibbon. (Anchorage Historical and Fine Arts Museum)*

"...we were routed out of bed, before breakfast, and we loaded a hundred and ten cords aboard and then went back down the river a short ways and loaded another sixty cords on the same barge. We were one tired bunch of guys."

High banks and low water made the job doubly difficult. Knutson writes, "The problem was how does a deckhand handle a load of cordwood down a steep plank when the load is behind him? The gangplank had a vertical piece of wood along the side . . . lined with a strip of hardwood called a 'rubber.' [It] allowed the truck wheel to make contact with the rubber at an angle and this served as a brake. I have seen men on all fours on the river bank with longshore truck and cordwood landing all around them. I have also seen men run across the bow of the boat and [been] pinned against the lifeline on the far side, pinned against the mast, the winch or whatever happened to be in their way."

Nulato prior to 1910. Garrett Busch and Alaska Commercial Company stores existed side by side, common practice in many Yukon villages. (University of Alaska)

Day Navigation Co. tugs and barges on the Iditerod River. These very shallow drafted vessels served the side stream mining camps for years before being sold to Black Navigation. (Arthur Peterson)

Rum Runners

Prohibition in Alaska, as in other parts of the country, wasn't much of a deterrent to sourdoughs who had been used to taking their whiskey when and where they liked. The steamboats coming down the Yukon from Canada were a prime source of supply.

As Knutson relates, "The deckhands would get old five-gallon cans filled with grease from the galley, bury two or three bottles of liquor in the grease, pack the cans ashore and sell the "grease" to the Indians for their dogs.

"Cliff Paul [another steamboat man], told of the time he had a man and wife with a sick child in one of his staterooms. Cliff had the child's bunk loaded with liquor underneath the mattress. The searchers very considerately elected not to disturb an ailing child."

Another plan involved a false top in the five-gallon coal oil can with about an inch or so of oil in the top. The rest—whiskey. There were also false bottoms in egg cases, kegs marked 'white lead' and kegs or bottles baled in hay.

"The Feds were using a large trunk for a work table to rest their paper work in Nenana when the chief steward told a couple of waiters, 'Boy, you guys were supposed to have had that luggage up to the hotel by now.' That luggage was whiskey trucked off in full sight of the Feds and delivered as ordered."

Weathering the Great Depression

Times were tough in the 1930s. All over the country the unemployed were standing in soup lines or selling apples on street corners. But on the Yukon the boats kept running. Traffic wasn't good, but it wasn't that bad, either.

According to Adriana Peterson, George Black's daughter, "Alaska always had a depression. In those days we didn't know the difference. People would go into business one summer and then they'd go out of business the next spring. My Dad would haul anything. The movie, 'Lure of the Yukon', was made on his boat."

The changes were gradual, but Yukon navigation was changing.

Fledgling air services were springing up. Bush pilots, some of them flying rickety planes left over from World War I, had begun flying passengers and cargo into remote locations heretofore reached only by boat. With no new vessels constructed in more than a decade, the sternwheeler fleet was aging. And, many of the experienced (and colorful) skippers and pilots were retiring and dying.

Names like Ralph Newcomb, John McCann and Ken McLees were still known in every village where steamboats docked, but the new breed brought in to fill growing gaps in their ranks weren't always the best recruits.

Referring to new captains and pilots the

Alaska Railroad had hired from the Columbia River, Knutson remarks, "Those Columbia River pilots aren't so hot when you put them up here on the Yukon where they don't have a buoy light every half mile or so. They [on the *Alice*] have been stuck several times this year where we [on the *Yukon*] haven't been stuck any."

Though the steamboats used the paddlewheel to flush the sand from beneath a stranded barge, just as the screw-driven boats do today, they had another technique for freeing the boat known as "sparring."

The sternwheelers carried long wooden spars leaning vertically against the front housing. When stuck on a sandbar, deckhands lowered one end of these spars to rest on the bottom while a large block and tackle was fitted to the upper end. A winch tightened the line on the top forcing the spar down and lifting the bottom of the boat

free. Then, either the paddlewheel was used for flushing, the boat slid sideways off the bar or, using the spars, the crew literally "walked" it over.

The 1930s saw a spate of new construction on the river. In 1933 the Alaska Railroad built and launched a big new sternwheeler, the *Nenana*, from their boatyard at Nenana. Weighing in at 1,128 tons and 236 feet long, she had the capacity to assume all duties from Nenana downriver to Marshall, while the *Alice*, AAR's other steamer, took over the run to Fort Yukon. Her launching was fortuitous, for the following year the federal government raised the price of gold from $20.67 to $30 an ounce, stimulating a boomlet of activity in the mining districts of the Yukon Basin.

British Yukon Navigation embarked on a building program in the '30s as well. The ore

Steamers General J. W. Jacobs *and* General Jefferson C. Davis *hauled out for the winter, October 27, 1922. Both had just been transferred to the Alaska Railroad. The photo was probably taken at Nenana. (Anchorage Historical and Fine Arts Museum)*

74

The spruced-up General Jefferson C. Davis *tied up along the middle Yukon, probably in the late 1920s. This vessel served the Alaska Railroad until 1933. (Adriana Peterson)*

business was picking up from Mayo and Keno Hill Mines on the Stewart River and riverboats were needed to carry it.

Up to this time, passenger traffic had been primarily residents or visitors traveling by riverboat to specific destinations. Alaska and the Yukon were too far off the beaten path and lacked the amenities to attract any but the most adventurous tourists. But in the 1930s the White Pass and Yukon began advertising and catering to the tourist trade. All took steamships to Skagway and rode the narrow-gauge line over White Pass. Some lingered at Lake Bennett or took a lake steamer on Taku Arm to wilderness lodges. Others visited Whitehorse and Dawson. But, thousands made the famous Circle tour, continuing down the Yukon by AYN steamer to Nenana, boarding the Alaska Railroad train for Mt. McKinley and Anchorage and returning by steamship to West Coast ports.

To handle the increased traffic BYN rebuilt the *White Horse* in 1930. In 1936 the company launched the *Klondike*, 210 feet long, followed by the smaller *Keno* (613 tons) and *Casca* (1,300 tons) in 1937.

Shooting the Rapids on the Upper Yukon

The new boats were better, faster and more maneuverable than their predecessors, but the hazards of the upper Yukon were still there and it took a skillful skipper to get them through in one piece.

Ice was always a problem. Knutson relates, "The river [Yukon] below the lake [Laberge, below Whitehorse] was free of ice about a month earlier than the lake so a crew could be brought in to provide service.

"Freight was transported across the lake ice with horses, caterpillars and automobiles. Many close shaves were caused by rotten ice.

In this scene from the winter of 1905-1906, at least seven sternwheelers are wintering in Dawson Slough near Dawson City. Pilot house windows are boarded up, but the second in line has a fire in her boiler. (Yukon Archives)

"A number of stories have been told about boats that were deliberately frozen in for the winter where shallow water would freeze them to the bottom. The ice could be thawed around the sides with steam, but there was a problem warming the bottom. The spring thaw would cause the water in the river to rise while the bottom was still frozen solid. Water would rise over the deck and flood the bilge, in effect sinking the boat right on the spot.

"One trip upriver through the lake without benefit of a barge in front, the *Yukon* suffered thirty-one broken ribs in the hull." Captains kept deckhands stationed in the bilges on those trips through the ice. "Under the pressure of the ice against the hull, one of the ribs would split lengthwise and then when the pressure was released the split would disappear. The split rib would be marked in yellow [carpenter's chalk] so

the shipwrights could sort out and replace the damaged ribs when port was reached."

Knutson also describes the technique of "lining through" the rapids on the upper Yukon. "One and one-quarter inch diameter wire cables were installed at the various rapids for those boats needing help from the steam winch to buck the current going upstream. The *Yukon* was powerful enough so that Hell's Gate was the only rapids that we had to 'line through.' We would approach the rapids from below and get in close enough to the bank so the slack in the cable, fastened to the rock above and below, could be picked up by the use of pike poles, then hauled by hand through snatch blocks and chocks, then onto the steam winch or capstan. We would take ten turns on the winch head and tighten up on the cable and then the *Yukon* just hung on the cable and the pull of the winch would help get us through. There were so many rocks in Hell's Gate that the pilot had much better control of his boat hanging onto the cable. Coming downriver you were on your own. The Canadian boats lined through most of the rapids going upriver."

The rapids claimed many a victim and damaged others in passing. "The port side of the *Yukon* was torn off in the spring of 1938, including a six-inch-thick guard rail, to within a hand's width of the hull about 2 a.m. on a real dark night. Women were screaming and the men probably would have had they dared . . . there was a long lineup to go to the men's restroom on the aft end of the observation deck immediately after the incident."

Two Newcomers Come to Stay

Two young men, Arthur Peterson and Allen Brown, came to the Yukon in 1938. Two who would remain and would participate in changing river navigation from a patchwork of steamboats and small operators into a modern transportation system.

Arthur Peterson, moved north to Alaska with his father at an early age, worked all over the territory in the 1930s and married George Black's daughter, Adriana. When Black secured the U.S. Mail contract between Nenana and Dawson in 1938, Peterson was the logical man to handle the new run.

Peterson, known along the length of the river as "Art", describes surviving his first season on the boats by "main strength and awkwardness." "George gave me a boat [the *Kusko*] and an Indian and a mail contract. The Indian was supposed to know the river. Well, I took him 100 miles from home and he didn't know any more than I did.

"We had three boats. George took care of the lower river [below Nenana] with the *Idler* and I took the upper river." (The diesel-powered *Idler* measured 62 by 18 feet; the smaller *Kusko* was 35 by 10 feet. Black also had another boat, the *Mud Hen*, measuring about 30 feet.) Peterson had a device on the *Kusko* that specially adapted the boat for shallow water. The propeller shaft

The 35-foot Kusko *plied the Yukon and side streams for years with Arthur Peterson as skipper for Black Navigation Co. The* Pelican *is tied alongside. (Arthur Peterson)*

By 1938 many of the Yukon's grand sternwheelers were lying rotting on this beach at St. Michael. The Sarah *and* Suzie *are derelict in background. (Anchorage Historical and Fine Arts Museum)*

was joined to a universal joint. In deep water the screw could be lowered below the hull for greater thrust, then tucked back up into the tunnel when shallow water was encountered. Peterson had one of the first Gemini diesels and later installed a General Motors truck engine and clutch that served as the inspiration for Gray Marine applications.

"George worked the side streams, mainly the Koyukuk. We had the mail contract between Nulato and Wiseman. We had to be careful not to get anybody mad at us or they'd load us down with a bunch of parcel post mail and we couldn't make any money."

Clyde Day, who had begun working with his father, Glenn Day, on the Iditarod River boats in 1935, recalls Peterson and his *Kusko*. "That little boat had lots of power, but no muffler. You could hear Art coming 100 miles away."

Mrs. Peterson Becomes a Trader

By the second season, Adriana went aboard the *Kusko* to cook for the two-man crew. "We spent a lot of time on the bars," she recalls. "The dishes would fly. I was about ready to run home after the first trip.

"We lived on corned beef, ham and canned wieners, shrimp and chicken. They had cold storage on the *Idler*. When we met it we'd restock our supplies."

After a few trips, Adriana decided to go into the trading business herself. "We'd pull into these small villages with the mail and someone was always asking me to bring them this or that. Art was selling gas and groceries, so I got a peddler's license and began selling things. I'd take orders for everything from dress material to kitchen utensils, then get the goods on consignment from Nenana and deliver them the next trip. I made a little money from it, but more importantly, it was a good way to become friendly with the Natives.

"In the fall of the year the Natives would go to their home cabins scattered throughout the country. They'd trap for fox, marten and other animals then come into a trading post just before Christmas, trade their furs, buy groceries and hang around until after New Year's. Then they'd return to their home cabins and trap until just before breakup.

"The Rat Dance signaled the spring muskrat ['rat'] trapping season. When we went upriver in the spring, we'd pick them up all along the Yukon and take them in to Steven's Village, Fort Yukon or other stops where they'd trade their fur. We'd bring out furs from the trading posts for shipping.

"About the 4th of July they'd set up their fish camps along the riverbanks and fish for salmon until September.

"There's nothing quite so lovely as drifting down the Yukon on a moonlight night past the fires of the Indian fish camps out in the middle of nowhere."

Alvina Brown (Mrs. Allen Brown), who worked in the post office at Nenana, remembers another side to the Petersons' fur hauling business. "I used to hate to see Art Peterson coming," she says. "He'd bring in those stinking old muskrat pelts (as well as pokes of gold) to be mailed. We couldn't get the smell out of the post office for weeks."

Allen Brown came to the Yukon River in 1938 as well. Brown had been working in a creamery in a small town in Oregon when one of the Alaska Railroad's captains recruited him to go north as a deckhand the following summer.

While in Nenana waiting to go aboard the *Alice,* Brown was pressed into service as a waiter in the company dormitory and relates a tale typical of the wild and woolly days of steamboating.

"Those old captains were pretty tough to deal with. They demanded a lot and gave you a rough time when you didn't perform. Anyway, one night one of them ordered his steak well done. I delivered it, but he wasn't satisfied. He sent it back to the kitchen, not once, but twice, saying he wanted it done more. Well, after the third time, the cook got fed up, threw the steak on the floor of the kitchen and stomped on it. 'There', he says,

Black Navigation Co.'s Idler *tied up along the Chena River near Fairbanks. Light planes such as this one began flying mail and express in the 1930s. (Arthur Peterson)*

'that'll fix him!' You know, I took that steak back to the captain and he ate it right down without a word.

"Ever since then I've never had the nerve to cross a cook."

Strange Tales are Told. . .

Robert W. Service has written:

"There are strange things done in the midnight sun
By the men who moil for gold
The Arctic trails have their secret tales
That would make your blood run cold. . ."

But the miners weren't the only ones with their strange tales; the rivermen had them as well.

Al Brown relates the bizarre incidents following the freezing-in of the *Alice* in 1940.

"We froze in at Crossjacket that winter. The next spring they had to fly us in to cut the ice around the boat and float her free. The bush pilot could only get us onto a sandbar about 25 miles below the *Alice*. Three of us, myself, a deckhand and a cook, hiked all those miles in one day.

"Well, this cook kept wanting to get into the water [leads next to the bank] and get out on the ice in the middle of the river. I told him no, it was too dangerous. Then when the ice began to break up, I was sure the boat was going to sink. Big chunks were coming down that slough, banging into that wooden hull. Two of us collected some food and went ashore, but that cook insisted on staying aboard no matter what happened.

"I thought it was a little strange he wanted to stay aboard that boat, but then in the middle of the summer we were making a trip down the river and we tied up for lunch down below Hot Springs. We were all sitting there eating and suddenly heard a splash. We ran outside and there was the cook swimming around the boat.

"On the next trip we'd tied up for the night and, next morning, the cook wasn't there for breakfast. We hunted and blew the whistle for hours, but couldn't find him anyplace. So we went on down the river, unloaded our load and were heading back up when we spotted him on the bank at Hot Springs. His shoes were completely worn through and he'd had to hike many miles and swim at least two sloughs to get from where he disappeared to where we picked him up.

"But that isn't the end of the story. On the next trip we'd tied up again for lunch when we all heard a splash. We ran outside and there was his cook's hat floating on the water. We never saw him after that."

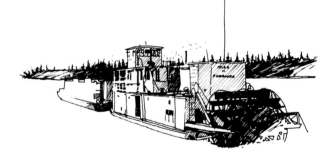

VII

THE WAR YEARS
1941-1945

British Yukon Navigaton Co.'s White Horse *and* Klondike *docked at Dawson with barge loads of Army vehicles and construction equipment for Alaska Highway. (Yukon Archives)*

The War Years
1941–1945

Alaska and the Yukon Territory were totally unprepared for World War II. Despite numerous warnings by such prominent military experts as Brigadier General William "Billy" Mitchell that Alaska would be a prime target in a Pacific war, government and the military dragged their respective feet. On the eve of the conflict the only military establishment in the territory was Chilcoot Barracks at Haines, garrisoned by 11 officers and 300 men armed with obsolete Springfield rifles.

Funds had been appropriated to construct a "cold-weather testing station" for aircraft and materials at Fairbanks (Ladd Field). The Navy had begun construction on two air stations at Sitka and Kodiak and had completed bases for seaplanes and submarines at Kodiak and Dutch Harbor by the time of the attack on Pearl Harbor on December 7, 1941.

The transportation system was impossible. A handful of sternwheelers and small screw boats plied the Yukon River and its tributaries during the summer. The single-track Alaska Railroad served Fairbanks year around, and the narrow-gauge White Pass and Yukon kept supplies flowing to Whitehorse, but the rest of the interior was isolated for eight months of the year. No highways connected the interior towns and the few scattered commercial landing fields made travel by air tenuous at best.

Obviously, if our far north frontiers were to be defended, supply lines had to be improved. And, in a hurry.

The Alcan Highway

The first big project aimed at opening up the north was the Alcan Highway. An all-land route to the interior had been proposed for more than two decades; construction only began on the route in March 1942. Eight months and 11 days later, 11,000 Army Engineers had punched a 1,420-mile road through the wilderness. The Alcan Highway (now the Alaska Highway) connected Fort St. John in northeastern British Columbia with Fairbanks via Whitehorse.

In June of the same year engineers began work on a 500-mile pipeline connecting oil wells at Norman Wells, Northwest Territories, with a refinery at Whitehorse. A third transportation project, surveyed but never built, was the Trans-Canadian, Alaska and Western Railroad to connect Canadian rail lines at Prince Rupert with ports on the Bering Sea.

Sternwheelers of the American Yukon and British Yukon Navigation Companies were nearly totally committed to two of these projects. Con-struction equipment, vehicles, gasoline and the groceries and supplies necessary to support the army of road workers on the northern end of the Alcan Highway came over the WP&Y railroad to Whitehorse. Lake steamers delivered them to construction camps on the headwater lakes. The *Keno, Klondike, Aksala, White Horse* and *Casca* carried mountains of material up the Teslin River as well as other side streams and plied the Yukon and Tanana to Fairbanks. The *Yukon* transported men and equipment, including horses and mules, involved in the railroad survey.

All during the war, the steamboats were in nearly constant use. Poorly maintained and pushed to their limits, they were in deplorable condition by war's end. At the same time they were helping to construct the highways that would eventually put them out of business.

Sternwheeler Yukon, *flying the flag of the American Yukon Navigation Co., was a mainstay of river service for the military in World War II. (Arthur Peterson)*

The little Taku Chief *was operated by the Civil Aeronautics Administration during World War II and at retirement was placed on permanent display at Nenana. (Arthur Peterson)*

Lend-Lease to the Soviets

Beginning in 1940 the Civil Aeronautics Administration (CAA) built a number of auxiliary airfields in Alaska in support of the military. With the advent of war, fields at Galena, Bettles, Birches, Lake Minchumina, Kaltag, Ruby and other places in the interior became important on the lifeline to the Soviet Union.

In 1941 the Army Ferrying Command established an all-air route to deliver the hundreds of bombers and fighters being supplied to the Soviets. Taking off from Great Falls, Montana, pilots hedgehopped across northwestern Canada to Ladd Field at Fairbanks and later to the airfield at Galena. Here, Soviet pilots took over the planes, flew to Nome and then across the Bering Strait to Siberia.

Al Brown, by 1941 pilot of the *Nenana*, recalls the decision to build the field at Galena. "We took the first load on the *Nenana* that they intended to build Galena with—cats, lumber, earthmovers, trucks and engineers. They were going to build it down below Bishop Mountain. That's about 30 or 40 miles below Galena. We unloaded all their gear there and then we went on to Marshall.

"They took the cats and dozed off the tundra and when they did, they had nothing but ice, of course. It started melting and they just had a big

84

The handsome Nenana *(shown here on her last voyage at Beaver) was built in 1933 for the Alaska Railroad and became the flagship of the Yukon River fleet until retired in 1957. She's now a museum in Alaskaland Park in Fairbanks. (University of Alaska)*

Pilot's-eye-view from the wheelhouse of the Yukon. *This sternwheeler saw service in World War II transporting men and materials for the still-born Trans-Canada, Alaska and Western Railroad from Prince George to the Bering Sea. (Arthur Peterson)*

loblolly. Well, one of the engineers went to Galena for the mail and saw how nice and level the area around the town was, so they loaded everything back on the boat and we took them up to Galena.

"Everybody told them Galena flooded, but they weren't paying any attention. Well, a couple of years later, along comes a big flood and wipes everything out."

In addition to the equipment brought in, the Army picked up every piece of machinery they could find to build and operate Galena. Much of it came from the mining operations along the side streams.

"The military came in and contracted with us [Day Navigation] to haul equipment—drag lines, cats, loaders—from those mining sites and take them up to the airport," says Clyde Day.

"We were hauling fuel and supplies from Nenana down to Galena with the big boats and going up the Koyukuk, Kantishna and Iditarod with the small boats to haul mining machinery. The whole job took about two years and it pretty well put the miners out of business for good."

The Independents Get a Shot in the Arm

The war was a boon to the independent rivermen. More general freight, construction equipment and petroleum was pouring into Nenana than the Alaska Railroad boats could handle. Everything that would float was being pressed into service.

"All of the aviation gas, diesel and other petroleum products were shipped in 55-gallon drums, back then," recalls Art Peterson. "There were no bulk oil barges. Thousands and thousands of

86

these barrels were piled all over the dock at Nenana.

"The Alaska Railroad boats couldn't handle the volume so the Army would make a bunch of these barrels into a raft to float them down the river. They'd hire anyone who had even just a little kicker boat to push them down to Galena. If the boatman made it and delivered the barrels, he got paid. If he didn't, he just turned around and came back for another load.

"Many of them didn't make it. They'd lose the raft on a bar or the raft would break up in the current. Or, they'd get into a dead end and those little kickers weren't powerful enough to back them out. For years afterward there were barrels scattered over every sandbar and slough between Nenana and Galena."

George Black and others were getting all the cargo they could carry and, because space was at a premium, they could command rates that would bring them a healthy profit.

Art Peterson was still taking the mail upriver, but the route now terminated at Eagle, the last village before entering Canada. Business was so good hauling gasoline and freight for the Army, Peterson chartered Lon Brennan's biplane to fly the mail and release the *Kusko* for more profitable work.

"I could cover the whole mail route in one day," says Peterson. "When I submitted the bills to the Post Office Department, they couldn't figure out why all of them were signed on the

The Hazel B No. 1, *here on the beach at Galena, came from the Stikine River to the Yukon to aid in hauling the heavy military traffic during the war. (Clyde Day)*

same date. The next time the contract came up for renewal, the service by air was in it. Today, it's all done by air."

To supplement the Yukon fleet, the Army acquired two boats from the Stikine River, *Hazel B I* and *Hazel B II*. Sid Barrington, who owned both of them, operated *Hazel B I* under contract and later leased the *Aksala* from BYN. The Army placed a military crew on the *Hazel B II* and hired Jimmy Binkley, who had previously worked for Black Navigation, to skipper the boat.

According to Clyde Day, a problem arose because Binkley had joined the Army Air Corps. "There were only about 12 of us guys left who really knew the river. Binkley was needed to run boats, but the Air Corps didn't see it that way. They were constantly threatening to put him in jail if he didn't return to duty and the military transportation people were always having to square it for him.

"I was in a similar position. My draft board was in Seattle and they were after me all the time while General Buckner [ranking officer of the Alaska Defense Command] was trying to keep me out of the Army so I could run boats."

The CAA River Transportation Unit also operated its own vessels during World War II serving airfields scattered through the interior, principally on the Kantishna and Koyukuk Rivers. They had acquired the *Taku Chief* from southeast Alaska and supplemented it with two small screwdriven "J" boats operating out of Nenana.

Others included Nick Dementieff (whose son still operates on the river), Don Peterson with the

Art Peterson, in command of the Kusko, *carried mail and military cargo to the new air base at Galena during World War II. (Arthur Peterson)*

The Taku Chief *on the ways at Nenana. With the end of the war this tug was transferred to the Alaska Railroad and then to Yutana Barge Lines. (Larry Shelver)*

diesel paddlewheelers *Emma R* and *Elaine G* and "Doc" Gordon with his home-built sternwheeler that "looked like an apartment house mounted on a barge."

In 1943 American Yukon Navigation sold five vessels and all of its routes in Alaska to the Alaska Railroad for $101,125.95. All Canadian operations on the American portion of the Yukon had now ceased. With the sale went the sternwheelers, *Julia B, Suzie, Schwatka, Seattle No. 3* and *Yukon.* Only the *Yukon* was fit for service; the rest were derelicts at St. Michael and Dawson.

The *Barry K,* a wooden-hulled 160-foot sternwheeler, also came to the Alaska Railroad the following season. She had been built in 1923 as the *Lewiston* and operated by the Union Pacific Railroad on the Columbia and Snake Rivers.

Life with the Military

In addition to carrying military cargo that constituted the preponderance of all freight on the Yukon during the war years, the Alaska Railroad was responsible for regular schedules from Fort Yukon down to Marshall. With rationing, groceries and commissary stores for the boats were scarce. Any change in subsistence diets was welcome.

Al Brown relates incidents aboard the *Nenana* during those years. "When you came down on the first trip in the spring, you always had a big load of mail, plus all kinds of fresh stuff. When the *Nenana* would pull into a village, all the miners, trappers and Natives were all right down at the landing because they hadn't seen anything fresh since freeze-up.

"During the war, all we could get in the way of meat on the boats was mutton. Everybody got fed up with eating mutton, mutton, mutton, meal after meal. One day we're going down the river and the mate, Al Larsen, came up to the pilot house and said, 'We've got to get something to eat besides mutton. How about if I get us some king salmon?'

"When we passed Pine Butte, I shut her [the *Nenana*] off and let her drift while Al negotiated with some Indians in a boat for some salmon. Well, the Indians piled a whole bunch of salmon on the deck and said they'd charge us four bits apiece.

"So Al says, 'How about some fresh meat?' He goes into the freezer and comes out dragging two whole muttons and threw them into the Indians' boat. By this time the purser had spotted him and came running down from the upper deck yelling, 'You can't do that, that's government property.' Well, the Indians were long gone and since the purser wanted the salmon just as much as the rest of us, he never said anything about it."

Most of the boats were manned by inexperi-

Disastrous 1945 flood at Galena inundated the townsite and made a shambles of the military air base. Clyde Day with Hazel B I *participated in rescue of soldiers from hangar roof. (Clyde Day)*

enced military crews, while veteran rivermen held the captain, pilot, engineer and mate positions.

"Most of them were pretty good guys," says Brown, "but they didn't care. One time we were offloading some beer at the warehouse in Nenana when I noticed these cans of beer floating down the river. I walked onto the dock and here were the soldiers wheeling hand trucks loaded with beer right over the end of the barge and dumping it into the river. It was too much trouble to push it up into the warehouse.

"Another time they loaded a jeep atop a bunch of oil barrels right on the front corner of the barge. I told the superintendent [of the Alaska Railroad], 'If we hit a sweeper, it's going to knock that jeep right into the river.' He said, "If you lose it overboard, don't even slow down. Just keep right on going.'"

Clyde Day remembers, "Galena was dry, but the military had booze and beer in their clubs on the base. One time the Alaska Railroad boat came in with a whole barge load of beer. Somehow about 200 cases of beer disappeared be-

Yukon flooded in 1945 at Galena behind a huge ice dam. Army used B-17s to blast the dam loose with thousands of pounds of bombs. (Clyde Day)

tween the riverbank and the base. About every Native in town was in jail that night as well as half the Army."

At the height of the lend-lease program there were from 150 to 600 Soviet pilots waiting at Ladd Field and Galena to take planes across the Bering Strait. "On some of these military runs to Galena, I got to know the Russian pilots pretty well," says Al Brown. "When those Russians flew out of there [to Nome and Siberia], they'd have those planes loaded down with all the American products they could carry—cigarettes, booze, canned goods, everything. I'd ask them, 'Why don't you take me on a ride over to Vladivostok?' They'd say, 'We'll take you for a ride, Brown, but we can't take you over the line.' They lost a few planes out there [ed. note: 133 planes were lost during the program], but the Russians wouldn't send anyone out to rescue the pilots. They just left them out there."

Disaster Strikes Galena

The warnings of flood potential given to the engineers who built Galena were finally realized in the spring of 1945.

Richard Mathews in his book, *The Yukon,* writes, "The [ice] dam that formed below Galena in 1945 was so sturdy that it barricaded the river for more than 24 hours and was dislodged only after a squadron of B-17s unloaded 168,000 pounds of bombs on it. The airfield there . . . was largely destroyed. To the inhabitants of the river below Galena the flood had its compensations, however, for it distributed a manna of lumber, boats, drums of oil, K-rations, even tinned candies, all along the way from the base to the Bering Sea [sic]. As of 1966, residents of Marshall, nearly four hundred miles downstream, were still digging drums of diesel oil from their sloughs."

Clyde Day, who was there, remembers, "We'd bought the *Hazel B I* and I'd gone down to Galena to get her ready for the breakup. The airport was built on a point and the ice was jammed up at Bishop Rock which is 12 miles below Galena. They were flying down there with 500-pound bombs and trying to bomb that ice dam out of there, but nothing happened. The situation was getting more and more desperate when they flew some 2,000-pound bombs up from San Francisco. When they dropped those big bombs, the *Hazel B I* jumped about three feet out of the water.

"When the ice began to break up, the Army cut a hole in the dike around the airport to let us through to keep from being crushed. We and a bunch of empty oil barrels floated right onto the runway. A couple of the little Army tugs weren't so lucky. They got caught in the flood and floated all the way down to the delta before they got stopped.

"There were about 250 soldiers sitting on the hanger roof with water and ice all around them. They'd been there quite some time with no food. We chugged right into the hanger to pick them up. Then, as the water went down, the Army cut a hole in the dike at the lower end and pulled us through. We took those soldiers out to the bank of the river where PBYs flew in to pick them up."

Many rivermen remember the war years with fondness. It was a time of excitement, hard work and long hours and relative prosperity for everyone. But it brought irreversible changes. Airfields were scattered all over the interior and the airplane would seal the fate of most of the riverboats and the companies that operated them. Highways now linked Fairbanks, Dawson and Whitehorse to the outside world and the riverboats they'd long depended on were fast becoming an anachronism.

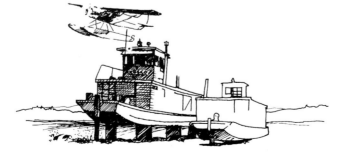

90

VIII

THE STRONG SURVIVE
1945-1982

With the slump in traffic after World War II, Alaska Railroad sternwheelers Yukon *and* Nenana *(shown here at Nenana) were sufficient for river service. (Anchorage Historical and Fine Arts Museum)*

The Strong Survive
1945–1982

The war was over. Elsewhere in the country pent-up demand for consumer goods was creating post-war prosperity, but along the Yukon things weren't so rosy. Military traffic, that had stimulated expansion of river freighting services, fell off abruptly. For the next five years Yukon boatmen would experience lean times, just another of the down cycles in the river's roller coaster economic history.

The Alaska Railroad, operating the *Alice, Nenana, Barry K* and *Yukon*, lost $171,054 in 1946, $191,624 in 1947 and $164,169 in 1948. In 1928 passenger business had grossed $20,365. By 1947 it had dwindled to a mere $4,000.

Ice proved troublesome to the AAR fleet as well. The *Yukon* was holed at Tanana in the spring of 1957, filled with empty oil barrels and towed back to Nenana to be repaired. That same winter, the *Nenana*, unable to make it back upriver to Nenana due to low water, froze in on the Innoko River but remained intact at breakup in the spring. The *Barry K* was damaged by ice the following winter. The *Hazel B I*, a former Stikine River tug acquired by the Army turned over to the Alaska Railroad, lost her power plant to ice two winters later (1949-1950). Hull openings had not been closed properly, allowing water to freeze in the engine and clutches, putting them out of commission for the following season.

But the loss of half the fleet during those years wasn't all that crippling. There wasn't much freight to carry anyway.

The independent operators who had prospered during the war were even worse off. Records indicate at least one operator was still tied to the dock at Nenana in mid-July one season waiting for his first load.

A Community of Friends

George Black and Art Peterson with the *Idler* and *Kusko* were still making a go of it. Art and Adriana now had a daughter, Artha, who accompanied them on their summer voyages to Fort Yukon.

Artha recalls, "My mother took me on the boats when I was nine months old. Our permanent home was in Fairbanks and when I was of school age, my mother would wait until school was out, usually by the first run of the season, then we would both go on the boat all summer."

"She would tie me so that I couldn't fall overboard. My favorite stop was Fort Yukon because there were lots of puppies there. I had friends all along the river, mostly Indians, and I'd go ashore to play with them."

Art Peterson, who probably counts more friends up and down the Yukon than any man living, explains the feeling of community that existed in those days. "The Yukon was more like a small town. Even though it might be nearly a thousand miles between settlements at either end, everybody was a neighbor to everybody else.

In the 1950s, the Alice, *nearing a half-century of service, handled most of the Alaska Railroad river traffic between Nenana and Fort Yukon. (Anchorage Historical and Fine Arts Museum)*

Oldtimers reminisce in front of the post office at Beaver. With a population of less than 100, Beaver, located 60 miles downstream from Fort Yukon, is typical of small villages along the Yukon. (Arthur Peterson)

We'd pull in and trade stories about people in other villages. Everyone would want to know how so-and-so is doing.

"Most of our friends were Natives—men like Timothy Wallace, Steve Matthews, John Sackett, Morris Thompson, Maury Smith. The Natives who worked on the boats sometimes had a little different style of looking at things, but we got along just fine.

"Take Dave Walker, for example. We'd be going down the river and if Dave saw a moose going across, he'd say 'the hell with the job and all the money.' He'd take off after the moose. That was his subsistance for the winter. It was important.

"Or, when we'd land in a village, Dave would disappear. For a long time I wouldn't find him because they [the Natives] wouldn't tell me where he was. I found out he had a trap line so I'd go and get him. That's all right because the next day he'd put in 18 hours working on the boat. It all evened out in the end and we just had to realize not all people look at life the same way."

The Yukon Traders

Northern Commercial Company with some 22 trading posts scattered up and down the river, dominated commercial activity on the Yukon in the early decades of this century. By the late 1940s the number of stores had dwindled; some had burned, some had been sold and the villages some served had just given up the ghost. Stores at Fort Yukon, Tanana, Ruby and several locations downriver were still flying the bright red and white flag above their doors, however. At Fort Yukon, trader Harry Cheek specialized in merchandising the intricate beadwork made by the Natives in the area while at the same time trading in furs and salmon and supplying some 300 Natives and 50 whites with groceries, clothing, hardware, produce and frozen meat. In addition, the store handled a busy mail-order business for remote villages away from the river.

Northern Commercial bought out its last competitor, Tanana Commercial Company, at Tanana in 1947. Manager Donald Humphries specialized in outfitting fur trappers in addition to his traditional grocery trade. The company actually went out of business for eight years during the Depression at their Ruby store, then returned to build a modest business in supplying miners with heavy equipment as well as groceries.

The small traders, like the small riverboat operators, were jacks of all trades. Dominick and Ella Vernetti operated the post at Koyukuk and had a brisk business in dried fish. Ira Wiesner, trader at Rampart, mined gold, ran a small cannery, a sawmill and the liquor store. Bill and Winifred Coghill, who operated the W.A. Coghill store in Nenana from 1916, grubstaked many a fur trapper for the winter. When the trappers brought furs in in the spring, an unwritten rule dictated the Coghills would pay half cash for the furs and the other half would go to pay for the trapper's grubstake.

The Coghills bought out the Northern Commercial store in Nenana in the 1950s. Native corporations acquired most of the rest, the last of which was the store at Fort Yukon.

Skeletons of the great paddlewheels that thrashed the Yukon for decades stand forlornly decaying on the beach at St. Michael in the 1950s. *(Anchorage Historical and Fine Arts Museum)*

Bill Yanert and his brother Herman were tourist attractions at Purgatory. Bill carved a huge devil figure out of wood and would raise it into a vertical position whenever one of the steamers carrying passengers was about to make a landing. A former surveyor, Yanert became known for his poetry and sketches published in a volume titled, *Yukon Breezes.*

A Decade of Change

The early 1950s brought big change to Yukon navigation. In 1950, the Alaska Railroad, tired of supporting a declining and money-losing passenger business, ceased to carry them aboard the two boats it was then operating, *Alice* and *Nenana.*

"But passengers and freight just didn't mix," says Al Brown. "We had to cater to passengers. Back in those days everyone [the officers] had to wear a uniform. Then maybe we'd get into Tanana, for example, and we had to post a notice what time the boat was sailing so passengers

In the fall twilight of an October evening in 1949, the Alaska Railroad's Nenana *shoves a barge load of cargo down the Yukon toward Marshall. (Anchorage Historical and Fine Arts Museum)*

could be back aboard. Well, we might get the freight off a couple of hours before the scheduled sailing time. Then, we had to sit around and wait, wasting time and money, until all the passengers were back aboard. Then, if it worked the other way, where we weren't through unloading by sailing time, the passengers would get upset."

By 1951 AAR freight had declined to just over 5,000 tons. CAA's River Transportation Unit, serving CAA installations on the Kantishna and Koyukuk Rivers, hauled more than 50% as much (2,598 tons) with the *Taku Chief* and purchased the small tug *Matanuska* from the railroad. Even though business was poor, AAR began exploring the possibility of purchasing two surplus stern-wheelers from the WP&Y or constructing two new tugs for the following seasons.

Black Navigation, then operating three boats—*Idler, Kusko* and *Pelican*—began the first of several expansions by purchasing Day Navigation. Among the floating inventory that went along with the sale, Black sold *Danaco No. 2* and barges to Nick Dementieff, retained the *Danaco Nos. 6 and 7* (boat and barge) and scrapped the remainder as being either unservicable or too small for use on the Yukon.

The year 1953 was to prove both tragic and momentous. George Black began the year by expanding his fleet with a new vessel, built at Fairbanks. The steel hull for the new *Yutana* (a

Yutana Barge Line's diesel-powered sternwheeler Yutana *spent several ignominious years as a ferry at Nenana before the present highway bridge was built. She's now the Fairbanks excursion boat* Discovery II. *(Yutana Barge Lines)*

96

Last active steamboat of the Canadian fleet, the Klondike *is towed along First Avenue in Whitehorse in 1966 to become a Parks Canada museum. (Yukon Archives)*

combination of the names Yukon and Tanana) was fabricated in Portland, then shipped north in sections by steamship and freight train. The 150 horsepower diesel and most of the machinery was salvaged from the old *Idler* to power the 80-foot vessel's sternwheel.

But George Black was not to live to see his dreams fulfilled. On the Tanana near Minto he fell overboard and drowned. Art Peterson says, "He was 59 years old and just worn out. We think he may have had a heart attack or stroke because he never struggled at all. We couldn't get the kicker boat started to go after him and when we did, he was gone."

Portland yards completed construction of the two big new diesel towboats for the Alaska Railroad in 1953. The *Yukon* under command of Captain William Maki and the *Tanana* under the command of Captain Howard L. Adams with Al

Brown as Pilot were towed north to St. Michael by the sturdy sea-going tugs *Quenett* and *Nez Perce*. Both of the new boats were all steel construction, 120 feet long and powered by twin diesels generating 1,200 horsepower. The *Alice*, now surplus, was sold to the mission at Holy Cross.

Romantic as the old sternwheelers were, Alaska Railroad crews were more than happy to see the new vessels arrive. Al Brown remembers, "These new boats made life a lot easier for us. They were only 120 feet long whereas the *Nenana* was 257 feet. Stick a couple of barges out front and you're talking about 400 feet. That much length is a lot more difficult to maneuver and get off of sandbars. A captain really has to be on the ball when turning that thing around. Then, too, the *Yukon* and *Tanana* had both main and flanking rudders and twin screws, giving you

Allen Brown, here at the controls of the Tanana, *came to the Yukon in 1938, piloted the* Alice, *skippered the* Nenana *to her permanent berth at Fairbanks and became senior captain with Yutana where he now serves as Port Captain. (Yutana Barge Lines)*

a lot more turning power at slow speeds. The only thing you could do with a sternwheeler that you can't do with these screw boats is back up for a long time. You could back the *Nenana* all day and still steer, because her main rudders were ahead of her wheel. But you could back the *Tanana* and *Yukon* just so long and, if they took a notion to turn around on you, you must just as well help because there was no stopping them."

While the big, powerful screw tugs were taking over the river, barges were evolving as well. Up through World War II, most barges had been wooden, many of them covered with large warehouse-type deckhouses. The new barges (two of them came north with the *Tanana* and *Yukon*) were all steel, low profile and compartmented to carry bulk liquid cargo.

By 1953 a new highway between Dawson and Whitehorse and a mine-haul road between Mayo and Whitehorse had doomed the BYN boats on

the upper river. The *Keno* had been laid up at Whitehorse in 1951, the *White Horse, Aksala* and *Casca* in 1952. Service below Dawson was discontinued in 1953 and most of the fleet was up for sale with no takers. That same year, the one remaining boat in service, the *Klondike,* was refurbished for the tourist trade. At a cost of $100,000 the company converted the boiler to burn oil, added additional cabins, a lounge and bar and enlarged the dining room. She would operate just two more years before being retired permanently. The steamboat era was drawing to a close.

Yutana Barge Lines is Born

Alaska Railroad's decision to get out of the river shipping business in 1955 took many observers by surprise. The railroad had been steadily losing money on its river operations for years, but just two years previously they had built two brand-new tugs and sent the *Nenana* to Whitehorse for extensive rebuilding, including replacing all of the deck and hull planking, plus a new paddlewheel and rudders. Correspondence of that period between railroad officials and Washington, D.C. administrators reveals the railroad went to great lengths to justify the very expensive rebuilding being done in Canada.

Art Peterson sheds some light on the subject. "The Alaska Railroad really didn't care much for the river trade. The through tariff from Anchorage or Seward all the way downriver to Marshall was only slightly more than the all-rail tariff to Nenana or Fairbanks. No wonder they were losing money; they were offering the river transportation almost free. I broke the tariff down and showed them what they should be charging."

Al Brown has another perspective. "The decisions were made in Washington. All the bureaucrats could see is that the operation was losing money. There was very little communication with the people on the river who could have told them how to fix it."

When the railroad put the river service up for bid, Art Peterson, Fred Goodwin (a Wein Airlines pilot) and Jack Bullock (who owned B&R Tug and Barge at Kotzebue) formed a partnership and submitted the winning bid. Under the terms of the agreement, AAR would continue to own the *Yukon, Tanana, Nenana* and *Taku Chief,* along with several barges, and lease them to the partners for a period of 20 years.

The new firm began doing business as B&R Tug and Barge, but within the year formed a new company, Yutana Barge Lines.

"We promptly raised the rates from next-to-nothing up to 88 cents per hundred pounds for the first 200 miles," remembers Peterson. "We weren't getting rich, but at those rates we could make some profit. We also turned the *Nenana* back to the railroad. With a crew of 35 she just couldn't pay her way."

After sitting idle in the Nenana River for two seasons, the steamer *Nenana* was given to the city of Fairbanks for permanent display in Alaskaland Park. In May of 1957, with Al Brown at the helm, she made her last voyage up the Tanana and Chena to retirement.

Two years previously, the last of the BYN boats, *Klondike* and *Tutshi*, had been retired. In 1960 the *Keno* made her last voyage on the Yukon downstream to Dawson for permanent exhibit. In 1966, Parks Canada moved the *Klondike* through the streets of Whitehorse and refurbished her circa 1937 as a steamboat museum. *Tutshi* is displayed at Carcross. Two other BYN boats, *Casca* and *White Horse,* had been saved from the scrapper for exhibit at Whitehorse, but on June 21, 1974 both were set afire by an arsonist and completely destroyed.

Thus, the steamboat era on the Yukon that had spanned nearly a century finally came to a close.

Peterson Branches Out

Salmon canning had long been one of Alaska's major industries but the big river and coastal canneries were dying out by the early 1960s. With an eye to new markets, Peterson, Bullock,

Pride of the new Alaska Railroad fleet, the twin-screw diesel tug Yukon *is launched from a Portland shipyard in the Willamette River in 1953. (Anchorage Historical and Fine Arts Museum)*

The two British Yukon Navigation Co. sternwheelers Casca *and* White Horse *had been preserved as museum pieces at Whitehorse when arsonists totally destroyed them on June 21, 1974. (George Tumpach)*

Arnold Akers and several others decided to go into the "mild cure" business, supplying salmon to Jewish consumers in the East.

Bullock and Peterson furnished the transportation with the old *Kusko*, one of the *Danacos* and several barges. Purchasing a warehouse at Marshall, and transporting surplus quonset huts and other military buildings down the Yukon, they established a fish camp in the delta, complete with electric generators, housing and a trading post. To preserve its delicate flavor, "mild cure" salmon must be chilled within hours after it is caught. Cutting ice from frozen delta lakes in the winter and preserving it with hay in the summer, they were able to process the fish immediately on-site where the Indians were fishing. Icing down the salmon in wooden boxes and collecting them on rafts, Peterson and Bullock then moved them to camp for cleaning and salting. Barge loads of barreled salmon were then shipped by sea or hauled by barge up the Yukon to Nenana and transshipped via the railroad.

Northern Commercial Company's branch still operated Alaska Rivers Navigation to serve customers in the delta as well as a small mild curing operation of their own. NCC's tug and barge operation, run primarily for the benefit of company trading posts, was losing money. Sensing an opportunity, Peterson secured a right-of-first-refusal offer from the company and, when the manager in the delta retired in 1965, purchased boats, barges and routes. The *Pat*, a tug that had been constructed from two former LCM hulls, took over the hauling chores from St. Michael into the lower river operating under the aegis of Black Navigation Company. The remaining

NCC boats, all of which were wooden, were scrapped at St. Michael.

Though Yutana had taken over all of the business formerly done by the Alaska Railroad, the company faced serious competition from one of the independents that had been founded during World War II.

"Weaver Brothers were really hurting us," relates Peterson. "They operated between Fairbanks and Galena. The military was giving them 50% of the oil business and that's virtually all they hauled. We had the other 50% of the business, but under the terms of our lease we also had to haul all the general deck cargo—the time consuming and less profitable part of the business.

"There wasn't enough for two companies to survive, so I told the military, 'Give all of it to one or the other of us.' We offered them a cheaper rate and would guarantee it. Weaver had only two boats and a couple of barges and couldn't handle the total volume the military required at that time. We could and we got the contract."

In 1968 Yutana purchased Weaver Brothers. Along with the sale went the *Kantishna* and *Rampart,* both excellent tugs.

A New Generation Inherits the Reins

Meanwhile, Artha, the Peterson's only daughter, away at the University of Washington, had met a young man who was destined to turn Yutana into a vigorous modern enterprise in the 1970s. Larry Shelver moved north to work on the boats in the spring of 1962; he and Artha were married the following winter.

Working part of the time on the company's ferries (the old *Yutana* and the *Cabna*) crossing the Tanana at Nenana (before the present high-

Still burning fiercely, the Yukon *is beached along the Tanana River on the morning after a mysterious fire erupted in her engine room and destroyed her. (Bob Bune)*

The White Horse *in happier days on the upper Yukon. During the last years before her retirement in 1952, she was the oldest sternwheeler on the river, having been built in 1901. (Yukon Archives)*

way bridge was built) and as second mate on the *Yukon,* Shelver learned the business quickly. But doing business on the Yukon was often as much who you knew as what you knew. Shelver remembers, "You just weren't anybody 20 years ago unless you'd been in the Scouts." [The Alaska Scouts had been an elite reconnaissance force that operated in the Aleutians Campaign during World War II.] "Wherever I'd go someone would ask, 'Who do you work for?' I'd tell them I worked for Bullock." [Bullock, Akers and others on the river had been in the Scouts.] "All of a sudden I could get anything I wanted—fuel, a place to stay, anything.

"Those first years I was on the boats we used to run all the way down to St. Marys and interchange with the boats coming up from the fish camp. We brought down all the supplies and salt for the next year and would load up with 1,500-

pound containers of fish. We kept them covered with burlap and watered down with sprinklers until we could get them back up to Nenana to load in refrigerated freight cars."

Realizing the need to make the business more efficient, Shelver took flying lessons, secured his pilot's license and convinced Art Peterson to buy the company's first plane, a single-engine Piper. Now, personnel, parts and supplies could be transported quickly between Yutana and Black Navigation's far-flung operations. When a problem arose that required a welder, an electrician or just on-the-spot decision making, Shelver could be there by air in a matter of hours.

By 1970 Shelver had spent a stint running Yutana's Galena operation and three years as the company's operations manager in charge of the dock and shops in Nenana. He had also acquired the Standard Oil distributorship in Nenana. In

Aging sternwheelers rest on the ways at Whitehorse in the 1950s. The Aksala *(formerly* Alaska*) appears to be partially dismantled, but the* Casca *and* White Horse *are intact. The stern of the* Klondike *is visible at right. (Michael D. Bradner)*

Flagships of the Yutana fleet, Tanana *and* Yukon *lie berthed together at Nenana. Moose antlers mounted atop the pilot house made the* Tanana *easy to spot. (Larry Shelver)*

the early 1970s, Art Peterson had acquired the stock of the remaining Yutana partners. After two years' absence in Washington State, running his father's business, Shelver returned to assume the position of general manager.

With a master's degree in petroleum transportation, a river pilot's certificate and an airline transport pilot's rating, Shelver was well qualified for the new responsibilities. He began innovating mechanized deck cargo loading as well as improved techniques for bulk fuel transfer and increased maintenance. Artha assumed responsibilities for financial management, record keeping and office management of both Nenana and Seattle headquarters. Peterson, the president of the company, was able to return to his first love, the river. He took over as master of the *Yukon.*

The following year, 1974, Shelver engineered the purchase of McGrath and Kuskokwim Freight Service, a barge line run by Harlan Eggleson on the Kuskokwim River. Yutana operated the service for three years with the tugs *Pat* (that had been resold to Eggleson), *Tammy,* *Little Joe* and *Chelan,* then sold it to John Binkley, transferring the *Pat* and barges to Black Navigation's St. Michael operation.

Rick Hoffman, Yutana's Operations Manager, recalls one of the more difficult spring seasons with the Kuskokwim boats. "The *Pat* had wintered in Steamboat Slough, just upriver from Bethel. Someone had forgotten to tighten the packing glands on the shafts when she froze in and the engine room filled with ice.

"We rode in in the spring by snowmobile in

the bank near Hot Springs on the Tanana and there is good reason to believe spilled diesel fuel came in contact with a hot engine. Within minutes she was enveloped in flames. Dave Walker, the pilot, had barely enough time to try the radio before smoke drove him out of the wheelhouse.

Yutana's office in Nenana had been shut for the night. No one answered the *Yukon's* distress call. But, far out in the Bering Sea, a tugboat captain picked up the SOS and radioed St. Michael. As fortune would have it, there was an all-night poker game going in the St. Michael office that night and the relay was heard. Employees at St. Michael telephoned Larry Shelver at his home in Nenana and rescue efforts got underway.

Al Brown recalls, "The *Rampart* was sitting there at the dock. Well, it was darker than pitch,

Larry Shelver, here in the cab of a dragline at Nenana, took over as General Manager of Yutana Barges Lines in the 1970s. (Bob Bune)

15-below weather to spend days chipping the ice out of the engine room by hand. The barges had frozen to the bottom and the tide was coming in to sink them. We frantically worked to free the barges, then spent another three weeks in freezing temperatures cleaning up the engine room."

That same spring the *Chelan* went down in a storm in Norton Sound and, if the *Pat* had not been there to pick up the crew, they probably would have perished as well.

The Yukon Comes to a Tragic End

Some rivermen swear the *Yukon* was haunted. Doors that were found open when they'd just been closed, footsteps on the deck at night, strange human-like sounds, shadow-like wraiths on deck and in the engine room convinced crewmen who served aboard her that there was something supernatural about the boat.

On one of the last runs in the fall of 1977, the *Yukon* mysteriously caught fire. She was tied to

Black Navigation acquired Day Navigation in the early 1950s and with the purchase came the Danaco *(several numbers) tugs and barges designed for extremely shallow side stream work. (Clyde Day)*

but we all climbed aboard, cast off the lines and the captain and pilot got us down there just shortly after dawn. We couldn't see our hands in front of our faces, yet that crew knew the river so well we made it without getting stuck.

"When we got there she was still burning furiously. Luckily all of the crew had gotten off without injury and were sitting on the bank waiting for us.

"That crew swears to this day they heard someone moaning in the flames. Yet they all got off OK. Maybe there was a ghost after all."

Yutana Moves into the '80s

"The loss of the *Yukon* really hurt us," says Shelver. "We managed to finish the season—just barely." The *Yukon* had recently been repowered and had been the most powerful tug in the fleet.

The loss had been felt, but the Yutana people soon made up for it with a rebuilding program. The fleet now numbered six boats—*Tanana, Rampart, Kantishna, Independence, Husky* and *Pat*. (The *Yutana* had been sold to Jimmy Binkley who rebuilt it as the passenger excursion boat *Discovery II*, operating out of Fairbanks.) The LCMs have been split lengthwise adding a new eight-foot midsection and a third engine. The result is a boat with more power and more maneuverability.

Shelver made other improvements as well. The St. Michael operation had always had personnel problems, primarily due to the isolation and difficult working conditions. Some personnel

were replaced and crews began coming down from Nenana on a regular basis. Maintenance, always a critical area, came in for its share of attention as well. Shelver soon brought on board Jerry Dana, an expert in diesel engines, to help manage the vessels.

As Yutana moved into the 1980s, it was a lean, efficient company providing vital services to all who live along the Yukon. Had he been there to see it, George Black would have been proud of his company.

On June 1, 1983, Peter Brix bought Sea Flight International, the holding company of which Yutana Barge Lines and Black Navigation are a part. Brix is a major stockholder in Knappton Maritime Corporation, a large tug and barge operator on the Columbia River, and operator of the Prince Rupert-to-Seward Aqua Train.

The sale is significant in that it brings increased capital resources to Yutana that will enable the company to improve service to interior Alaska as well as take advantage of opportunities to expand with the increased potential for mineral development.

Allied with Knappton, the company early in the 1983 season, transported one million gallons of less-expensive Puget Sound fuel to the mouth of the Yukon for distribution by Black Navigation vessels and substantial savings to the residents of the lower river.

Under the new ownership, Yutana and Black will continue to operate as independent companies, headquartered at Nenana, Alaska.

IX

120 DAYS TO DELIVER

Winter at Nenana. Yutana Barge Lines' boats Tanana, Yukon, Yutana, Taku Chief *and barges are tied up along the Nenana River. (Henry S. Kaiser, Jr.)*

120 Days To Deliver

Today, Yutana Barge Lines stands virtually alone as the single carrier on the Yukon River. To be sure, Jimmy Walker at Holy Cross, Claude Dementieff at Nenana and Roy Smythe at Fort Yukon operate small single tug and barge businesses serving the side streams and isolated settlements, but the vast majority of the work is Yutana's.

In the more than three-quarters of a century since the heyday of the steamboats, the river hasn't changed much, but the cargo, the hauling operation and the boat crews have. Where once the cargo was groceries and general merchandise, now it's bulk petroleum. Where loading and unloading of deck cargo was once accomplished with hand carts and muscle power, now it's done with forklifts and cranes. Where boat crews were once comprised of Natives and venerable captains and pilots, now the crews are non-Native; captains and pilots are virtually all under the age of 35.

Avgas, Diesel and Alcohol

The airplane has made the biggest difference in cargo mix. Larry Shelver explains, "When I first came on the river, we handled a lot of foodstuffs, carloads of canned milk, flour, potato chips, beer, soft drinks and thousands of cases of dog food. We handled a great deal of Sears mail-order business—lamps, kerosene stoves and barreled gas. Because there were no fuel storage tanks at the villages, there was very little bulk fuel. There was very little building material because there was almost no building going on.

"Then two things happened. Natives in the villages were switching from wood for heating to oil. Generating plants for electricity were being built that used diesel. And the villages were putting in bulk storage tanks. We began the change to barges that would handle bulk liquid cargo.

"At the same time, landing strips were being built at every little wide spot in the road. Airlines and air taxi services began to fly all the mail, express, and small freight such as mail-order packages from Sears.

The Yukon *under way with barges in tandem, a full load of petroleum and a light deck load somewhere on the middle Yukon. (Arthur Peterson)*

Kantishna *and barges ease away from the dock at Nenana to begin another voyage down the Tanana.* *(Larry Shelver)*

"Groceries dropped way off in the last five years or so because of the high cost of warehousing and heating warehouses. It's cheaper to fly in the supplies for the village trading posts on an as-needed basis than haul it all down the river in the summertime and store it all winter. Airplanes can operate in the winter, too."

But while the airplane has siphoned off much of the freight business that formerly went by riverboat, it has also been responsible, both directly and indirectly, for generating additional cargo that has more than made up for the loss. Military installations at Galena, Campion (just above Tanana) and Fort Yukon now account for

the majority of the business. Since statehood, and later, the creation of the Native corporations, new construction of schools, hospitals, generating plants, warehouses and other structures has added to the building materials and heavy equipment carried by Yutana.

"About 80% of our business is now bulk petroleum and related products," says Duane Benoit, Yutana's Administrative Manager. "We carry avgas (aviation gasoline), jet fuel, diesel and alcohol (for deicing aircraft and runways), plus lube oil, asphalt and other packaged petroleum products on deck. As a common carrier, we'll accept anything anyone wants to ship. We carry

Bulldozer prepares to launch the newly rebuilt In-dependence on the Nenana River at Nenana. (Larry Shelver)

The Tanana *underway on the Yukon with barge loads of military supplies for Galena. (Arthur Peterson)*

The Independence *was constructed right on the beach at Nenana in 1974 from an LCM hull. (Larry Shelver)*

Resplendent in a new coat of yellow and black paint, the Independence *prepares to pick up barges at Nenana. (Larry Shelver)*

pipe, lumber, portable housing, cars and trucks, dried fish for dog food, cranes, wrecked airplanes, anything."

The company has ten barges, seven of which are large standard-unit bulk carriers. Each can carry 12 different types of petroleum products. The city of Nenana owns the *Tanana* and several of the barges; the remainder of the boats and barges are company-owned.

In 1982 Yutana transported 33,162 gross tons of cargo; it was the company's third largest year. "There are ups and downs from year to year, depending on what's going on at the military bases and in the villages," says Shelver, "but, overall, the business is growing by about 5% a year."

Getting Ready for the Season

Yutana maintains two headquarters, one summer and one winter. During the operating season, the Nenana office is fully staffed leaving only one or two employees to answer telephones in the Seattle office. Since a great volume of the cargo originates or moves through Seattle (and Nenana is impossible in the winter), the company maintains an office there as a liaison to shippers that serves as operating headquarters in the off-season.

Shortly after the first of the new year, planning begins for the new season. Orders begin to trickle in from shippers. Equipment repairs are scheduled, replacement parts and supplies ordered. Officers and crew members who served aboard

Winter at Nenana sees Yutana Barge Lines' tugs buried in snow and ice. (Bob Bune)

Most tugs and barges are pulled onto the beach for the winter, making spring repairs and inspection easier. (Bob Bune)

Crewmen pile cargo high on barges leaving Nenana on season's first trips when the water is high. (Bob Bune)

the boats the previous year are asked to notify the company of their intention to return by March 1.

By the beginning of March things are moving north. Railroad flatcars loaded with spare engines, shafts, propellers, steel and spare parts for the boats and barges depart Seattle on the Hydro-train for Seward, where they'll travel to Nenana over the Alaska Railroad.

In mid-March welders and other ship fitting personnel begin to arrive at Nenana. The ground is still frozen, boats and barges are snow-covered, but the frantic preparation for the opening of the river, still two months away, gets rolling.

"When the boats and barges come in in the fall, they're either pulled out of the water or frozen in on the Nenana River," explains Al Brown, now Yutana's Port Captain. "Nothing is done to them except draining the lines and sealing them up for the winter. Everyone's tired and wants to go home.

"We only have 120 days or so to operate and we don't want any breakdowns if we can possibly avoid it. So, in the spring, we clean up the boats, go over the engines and generally get them in top working condition. Every boat gets new or reconditioned screws every spring.

"Boats and barges have to be inspected by the Coast Guard. All the barges have to be cleaned by hand. As a matter of fact, the Coast Guard inspectors tell us Yutana has the cleanest barges they've ever been into. Pumps and hoses have to be repaired and tested. Welders have to patch any holes in the decks or hulls.

"The work is hard. That steel is frozen and takes its toll of skinned knuckles and scraped skin. Joints and nuts are frozen and difficult to remove. Then, as it gets toward the middle of April, the days warm up, we get rain and the whole boatyard is a mass of slush. When we're working flat out everybody puts in ten or 11 hours a day, seven days a week. No days off."

New or refurbished propellers such as this one are fitted to each tug each spring. (Larry Shelver)

114

Tanana *(note yellow moose antlers) is eased down greased ways into Nenana River to begin season's service. (Bob Bune)*

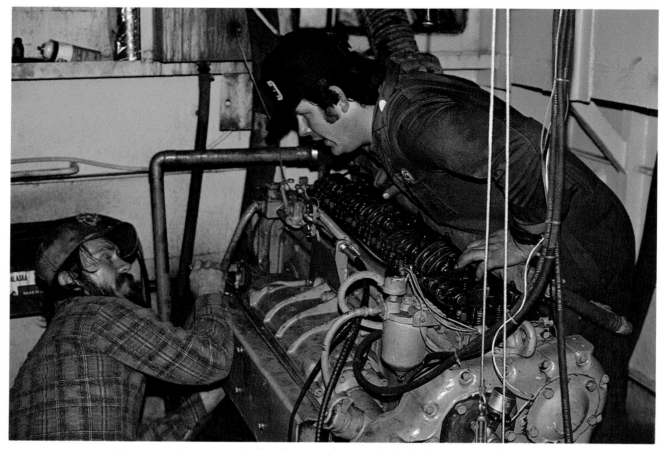

Yutana engineers repair diesel engine deep in the hull of the Pat. *(Bob Bune)*

By about the third week in April, boat crews begin to arrive at Nenana. They've hired at Nenana and live aboard whether the boats are high and dry on the beach or frozen in the river. Groceries and other stores, in refrigerated trailers or boxcars, arrive by rail. There are very few fresh fruits and vegetables available this early in the season. Auxiliary utility lines are connected to the boats to supply electricity and water; holding tanks take care of sewage.

Breakup

By May 1, everyone at Nenana is eagerly anticipating breakup. Freight trains are rolling into town regularly and long lines of tank cars stand on the sidings waiting to deliver their liquid products to the barges. Forklifts scurry around the yard, busily stacking great piles of pipe, lumber and other products that will become deck loads.

The Nenana Ice Classic, biggest ice pool in Alaska, signals the breakup. Ice in the Tanana didn't start moving until 5:36 p.m. on May 10 in 1982, somewhat later than normal. On the adjacent Nenana River, boats and barges frozen in all winter suddenly break free, leaving a perfect silhouette of their hulls in the fast melting ice. (Unlike the old wooden-hulled vessels, these steel boats and barges can withstand being frozen in.)

Crews maneuver boats and barges around to dockside on the Tanana where they can be loaded as quickly as possible to get a jump on the season that will last only 120 days.

Virgil Patterson, Yutana's Traffic Manager, is the best in the business. He learned his trade with the Alaska Railroad and is now responsible for making all that freight flow smoothly, including loading the boats and making the decisions as to who gets what, when. Years of experience, not computers, enable him to estimate almost to the pound how heavily a barge can be loaded and still make it down the river during low water.

"If the water ain't good," says Patterson, "you'd better not overload them or they're not

Welders replace screws on the Pat *that have been removed during the winter for refurbishing. (Bob Bune)*

Detailed inspections and repairs sometimes require cutting into hull and fuel tanks. This is the Tanana. *(Bob Bune)*

Empty gasoline drums are rolled and carried aboard barge from fish camp. Barreled fuel is delivered where bulk facilities are not available. (Bob Bune)

Forklift carried aboard the barge unloads barreled petroleum products at Fort Yukon. (Bob Bune)

going to get there. We can't load over four feet, six inches [draft]. Even four foot three is a little hairy; the crews don't like it. The ideal loading is between three foot nine inches and four feet.

"The last thing off is the first thing loaded. If you're going to go all the way to Marshall, then you put Marshall freight on first. At the beginning of the season we can carry more because the water is high.

"We have an early cutoff date of around August 15th when we don't accept any more freight. A lot of people don't understand that, but we have to stop about three weeks ahead of the last run to be sure we can get everything delivered. Our long time customers understand, but some of the new contractors think that if we've got a boat going out in September, they ought to be able to deliver in September. Then, it depends on where it's going. We might be able to squeeze in a late load for Galena or Tanana, but if the customer wants it delivered to the lower river, he's out of luck.

"We usually try to get all of the deck load on for a particular destination, then fill the load out with petroleum. We always have to carry some oil to get ballast for a top-heavy deck cargo."

Yard workers at Nenana prepare to place skids beneath tug before hauling her ashore. (Bob Bune)

Claude Dementieff's Romona *tied up at Nenana. Dementieff is one of only three independent operators on the river. (Barry C. Anderson)*

Autumn foliage is beginning to brighten the forests of the middle Yukon as the Tanana *makes one of the last voyages of the season. (Larry Shelver)*

The Husky *loads fuel from the tank farm at St. Michael for a voyage along the coast of Norton Sound. (Bob Bune)*

The 1982 Season

Yutana operated three boats on the upper river during the 1982 season, *Tanana*, *Rampart* and *Kantishna*, and two, *Pat* and *Independence*, on the lower river. The little *Husky* was kept in reserve. Departing Nenana, the *Tanana* headed for Fort Yukon, the *Rampart* and *Kantishna* for Galena. Newly rebuilt *Independence* sailed for St. Michael to relieve the *Pat* that had wintered there.

For the first time this year, *Pat* made five full-river trips, Nenana to St. Michael and return.

"In years past we used to have only two trips down there," explains Patterson. "We'd leave Nenana about the 1st of June and again about the 1st of September. Freight over the last couple of years has built up to where we'd have such a big load each time and in between the customers would just have to wait. We decided it would be a good idea to give them a little more frequent service, plus not such a big load each delivery."

Though the Tanana was ice free by the time the three tugs and barges departed Nenana, the Yukon was not. Great chunks of ice still moved down past the rivers' confluence and all three

On a bleak summer's day at St. Michael, Black Navigation tugs and barges lie offshore while awaiting assignment. (Fred W. Thomas)

The Tanana *and barges make their way up the Yukon in midsummer. (Larry Shelver)*

Tanana and barges unload deck cargo at Yukon fish camp. The main cargo, bulk petroleum, is carried in barge tanks and destined for villages and military installations. (Bob Bune)

Sunsets on the Yukon, which may occur around midnight, are one of the sublime rewards of a season's voyages. (Bob Bune)

vessels were forced to tie up to the bank just above the mouth of the Tanana and wait it out for four days.

Yutana's aviation capability gave them a decided advantage. Each morning General Manager Jerry Dana took off from Nenana in one of the company's single engine aircraft and headed down the river. Flying low over the moored tugs, he established radio contact, then turned and flew up the Yukon as far as Rampart. Checking on the ice (which was out of sight to the boat crews), he'd return to the boats and report his estimate of the situation by radio. When ice in the Yukon had finally diminished enough to make it safe for navigation, boat crews knew it hours before they could have determined it by sending a kicker boat down around the bend and into the Yukon.

Back in 1906, crew members from the ill-fated *Columbian* that had been ripped apart by a dynamite blast were forced to walk and paddle upriver for days to bring help to the injured.

That's not likely to ever happen again, for these days there's radio communication. All of Yutana's boats have two—one for communicating with the pilot boat; the other to talk to base at Nenana or St. Michael. Captains make frequent radio checks giving their position, partially for safety's sake, but also to let Nenana know whether they're on schedule or not. Though reception is sometimes poor, no boat is out of touch for very long.

Black Navigation and St. Michael

Black Navigation operates out of St. Michael in the summer months, serving nearby coastal communities, plus villages at the mouth of the Yukon. Black and Yutana are jointly owned, share tugs, barges and personnel. Virtually all of the traffic through St. Michael is bulk petroleum brought in by tankers from Dutch Harbor.

During the summer of 1982 the *Pat* began the season at St. Michael, then traded off with the *Independence* that became the single permanent

Rough seas in Norton Sound make fuel transfer a hazardous affair. The ocean-going barge has come from Dutch Harbor and is delivering fuel to a Black Navigation barge. (Bob Bune)

Crewmen negotiate a slippery deck and high waves to secure lines on the Black Navigation Barge, OB-6, to the tug. One mistake and a deckhand can easily be crushed between the barges. (Bob Bune)

Deckhands secure tarpaulins over perishable cargo to protect it from Yukon's summer rains, spray from surface. (Bob Bune)

tug based there. Understandably, St. Michael is not the company's favorite duty station and Rick Hoffman, Yutana's Operations Manager, flew down from Nenana periodically during the season to supervise the company's two permanent boatyard employees and the loading of barges.

The St. Michael operation differs considerably from the river operations. Breakup in Norton Sound comes late, typically at least three weeks after the ice has gone out of the middle Yukon. Tugs and barges are dependent on tides that run four to six feet to get onto the beach or into the mouths of coastal rivers. And, sudden storms can wreak havoc on boats and schedules, for there is virtually no protected water along this coast.

At Unalakleet captains must wait for high tide to make it over the river bar. Shaktoolik presents another problem. Here, barges are landed on the beach at high tide and fuel pumped to storage

above the high tide line. If the crew is pumping and the tide goes out, they must leave the barge and retreat to deep water. Elim, Koyuk, Moses Point, Egavik, Stebbins, Kotlik and the other coastal villages each have their own peculiar problems. Because Standard Oil divides the river and coastal jurisdictions at Marshall and most of Black's bulk deliveries are for that company, the St. Michael tug enters the mouth of the Yukon to deliver at Emmonak, Alakanuk, Sheldon Point, Mountain Village, St. Marys and Pilot Station.

In September two barges broke loose in one of Norton Sound's frequent storms and were driven on the rocks and sustained some bottom damage. That same storm forced the *Independence* to cruise around for three days before the weary crew could moor her.

Black Navigation crews are fond of telling one story of a storm that blew a barge loaded with fuel out of the bay one dark night about ten years ago. The barge was never recovered. Ironically, it was named *Romanoff* and the boatmen figure it probably blew all the way across to Siberia.

It's a Young Man's Life

The typical riverman has changed over the years along with the vessel he works. Except for Dave Walker, Yutana's senior pilot, and two of the three single-boat independents, the Natives are gone. All of the captains and all but one of the pilots are under 35. Deck crews are typically in their early 20s with some new hands each season fresh out of high school.

Yutana averages about 85 employees during the season with a 1982 annual payroll of $1,951,303. Employment peaks at about 100 during the short-term pre-season buildup of welders and shipwrights.

For the cadre of career captains, pilots, mates and engineers who return year after year, life on the river is a seasonal affair. Virtually all have homes "outside" where they spend October through March. Some take other jobs during the winter; others manage to live off the wages they make during the summer.

Though some years turnover in deckhands and cooks is high, Yutana has no need to advertise for help. More than 70% of new-hires have been referred by a friend; the remainder make applications by mail or just show up at the office in Nenana.

Surprisingly, few skilled men make the transition from the Mississippi or Ohio Rivers to the Yukon. Duane Benoit explains, "The Yukon is like no other river system. The skills learned on other rivers just don't apply here. We can train a smart deckhand to be a pilot just about as quickly as we could a pilot who had come from the Mississippi or Ohio."

"Turnover seems to follow economic cycles. If the economy is bad and jobs are scarce, as they are now, we may have a summer where we don't lose anybody. On the other hand, we've had seasons where every deckhand and cook has been replaced two or three times.

"The reason we lose first-year people is the nature of the job. There are no days off during the season and no place to go to have a good time even if there were. At least 50% of our first year losses are due to the girlfriends they left behind.

"But it's worthwhile for those who stay. If they come back the second year, they get a sizable increase in pay. People who work out well move up the ladder pretty fast."

Another Successful Season

By the last week in September, the *Pat* had come upriver for the last time and the *Tanana* had managed to get over the low water at Squaw Crossing on her last trip from Fort Yukon. The season had been a busy one with Yutana's five tugs making a total of 45 round trips. There had been no major mishaps and no freight was left standing in the Nenana yard.

The Nenana shipyard had been busy as well. Al Brown and his crew had completely rebuilt the *Independence* and had started work on rebuilding the *Husky*, a job that would be completed next year. Carpenters had constructed a new bunkhouse that would house crews next spring before the boats were launched.

Tired crews, eager to get home, hauled boats and those barges that required inspection up greased skids to resting places on the beach. Propellers were removed, lines drained, hull openings sealed and as each boat was put to bed for the winter, crew members headed for the Fairbanks airport and the flight home.

X

CAST OFF ALL LINES

The Tanana *is moored to the beach at Tanana on a bright summer day in August 1982. Outrigger planks are used by forklifts to unload deck cargo. (Barry C. Anderson)*

Cast Off All Lines

Slanting shafts of golden yellow sunlight glint off window panes and bounce off the corrugated metal Yutana warehouse and the buildings of Nenana Fuel's terminal. It's 5 a.m. on August 1, 1982 and most of Nenana still slumbers.

Down on the riverfront, the muted throb of diesels breaks the stillness. Yard crews have finished and the big barges, *OB-4* and *Stewart*, lie snubbed against the pilings, filled with petroleum and mounded high with freight for Tanana, Campion and Galena. Up ahead, the *Kantisha* lies tied up and silent, her crew still sleeping after the long voyage from Fort Yukon and a late night arrival.

The diesels belong to the *Tanana*, flagship of Yutana Barge Lines' towboat fleet, preparing to get underway down river on this, her seventh voyage of the season. Biggest of the Yutana boats and a sister of the ill-fated *Yukon* whose burned-out hull lies on the beach nearby, the *Tanana* is a luxury vessel by Yukon standards. Crew and officer quarters are comfortable and spacious. The galley is large and she includes two mess rooms (though only one is used for dining), several heads with showers and plenty of deck space. Unlike the smaller boats of the Yutana fleet, there's ample room for crew members to seek privacy on the long, confining days and

The Tanana *makes her way toward Fort Yukon. Ahead lies the Yukon Flats and many hours of groping through false channels, sandbars and marshes. (Bob Bune)*

The Tanana *is tied up along the banks of the Tanana just above the confluence with the Yukon on her first trip of 1982, waiting for the ice to melt. (Barry C. Anderson)*

Captain Keith Horton manipulates twin throttles and quad rudder tillers in the wheelhouse of the Tanana *to maneuver around sandbars. (Bob Bune)*

nights on the Yukon. Her bluff-bowed hull is painted black, her superstructure white with blue and yellow trim. A pair of big, yellow moose antlers mounted above the pilot house give her a rakish appearance.

Deckhands cast off the lines while up in the wheelhouse the Tanana's pilot, Charlie Hnilicka, moves the boat into position behind the leading barge. Rolling by in a great flow of muddy, slate-gray water, the Tanana River sucks and tugs at boat and barge with six knots or more of current. "The current here near the dock is tricky," explains Hnilicka. "You just have to take it slow and easy. You ought to see Dave Walker [pilot of the *Kantishna*] handle these barges. He's a real maestro."

Jockeying throttles and the two sets of dual rudder tillers, Hnilicka moves the leading barge back alongside the barge still tied to the dock, then moves the *Tanana* into position centered behind both. Barges and towboat are lashed securely together and the crew retires to the

Pilot Charlie Hnilicka speeds past the Tanana *in the pilot boat before reversing and tracing a route for tug and barges to follow through Squaw Crossing. (Barry C. Anderson)*

Deckhand delivers small bulldozer to customer at Galena. Agent Archie Thurmond unloads deck cargo here with shore-based crane. (Bob Bune)

messroom to fortify themselves for the long day ahead.

Breakfast this morning is ham, bacon, eggs, hash browns, French toast, fruit juice and coffee —all you can eat. Hnilicka explains, "This first day going down the Tanana is rough on everybody. We won't tie up until 10:30 or 11 o'clock tonight, if we're lucky. You really need full meals to make it through the day."

Talk at the breakfast table centers around who accomplished what on this latest trip to town. Amorous conquests, binges and just raising hell are the favorite subjects of bragging, kidding those who didn't fare so well and making plans for the next time in port. During the short summer season, Yutana crews work nearly continuously. Boats tie up in Nenana just long enough to fuel, restock stores and load cargo before sailing on another round trip. The pace is tough on crews and the infrequent opportunities to blow off steam are welcomed enthusiastically.

Because she's larger than the rest, the *Tanana* is manned by a larger crew. Twelve regular crew members make up her complement. This trip the Captain is Keith Horton; the Pilot, Charles Hnilicka; First Mate, Wayne Pattee; Second Mate, Troy Dana [son of Yutana's General Manager]; Chief Engineer, Lew Towne; Second Engineer, Jeff Hodge; four deckhands, Pat Kelly, Michael Lee, Joe Bailor and Mark Boehm; Cook, Margaret Garrett; and Stewardess, Eunice Lilly.

From Diesel to Datsun

Drawing 4.1 and 4.2 feet of water, barges *Stewart* and *OB-4* are loaded to capacity. The river is low by midsummer and if they settled just another few inches in the water, they'd be certain of stranding on the Tanana's sandbars. As it is, it will be touch and go in several places.

The cargo list reads like that of a floating hardware store. The *Stewart* is carrying 438.69 tons including 98,035 gallons of "Diesel Fuel

Remains of huge sternwheel are all that is left of two sternwheelers and three barges that blew ashore and stranded in tundra swamps near St. Michael. (Arthur Peterson)

Sternwheelers J. P. Light, New York *and one unknown vessel, plus barges carrying flour, were driven ashore in a storm about ten miles south of St. Michael in the 1930s. Remains of boats were still visible in 1982. (Arthur Peterson)*

Arctic" in bulk tanks destined for the military transportation officer at the Campion radar site. Perched on her decks for offloading at Tanana are:

  7 bundles timbers
  4 bundles plywood wallboard
  2 bundles sheetrock
  3 pallets roof paper, chimney and misc.
21 crates doors and misc.
  2 bundles roofing
  4 bundles ridges
  3 boxes building accessories
  1 box tempered glass
  6 crated snowmachines [snowmobiles]
  1 pallet shingles
  5 tanks propane
10 games and sets [for the Tanana Head
      Start Program]
  3 cartons mufflers

The *OB-4* carries another 98,207 gallons of diesel for Campion, plus Galena cargo:

   3 skids poles
   4 bundles aluminum siding
   1 skid culverts
 24 pallets insulation
   9 skids poles
   8 skids plywood
   3 skids mortar mix
   1 pallet sealer
122 drums paving
   4 drums lube and asphalt
 19 skids fencing and gates
   5 skids aluminum siding
 18 bundles pipe
   4 pallets fence fittings
 16 rolls wire
   6 bundles rods and bars
   8 bundles building materials

1 pallet nails
1 bundle insulation
1 bundle trusses
70 tanks propane
1 sander unit and 1 screen
111 pieces of miscellaneous cargo

Riding on the decks of the two barges are a Toyota pickup (with load), a Ford pickup, a dozer loader and a Ford Bronco. They'll be driven off under their own power at Tanana and Galena.

The Tricky Tanana

For the first couple of dozen miles of the 192 between Nenana and the confluence of the Yukon, the Tanana is deceptively tranquil. The flat, gray river of mud flows inexorably toward the sea, broken here and there by small islands and bars sticking above the surface. Sub-arctic forest of spruce, birch and alder stretches away to low hills in the distance. Undergrowth of willow, prickly rose, berry vines and thick shrubs is such a dense tangle it would be nearly impossible for a man on foot to move more than a few feet from the banks.

Here and there Indian fish wheels turn lazily with the current. Their large wire baskets scoop silvery salmon from the river and dump them onto a slanting trough where they slide down into a holding net or catchment tank. Occasionally, a drifting plume of smoke marks the crude shelters of an Indian fish camp where racks of bright red salmon hang drying and Indian women and children wave to the passing *Tanana*.

The *Tanana* hasn't encountered extreme shallow water yet, but floating logs, cut from the banks by the current, are a constant hazard. Entangle one in a propeller and it can put a boat out of action pretty quickly. Wayne Pattee, the First Mate, tells of a recent voyage when the *Kantishna* bent a prop on a floating tree. "It sure

Boilers, Pittman arms and other hardware from the sternwheel fleet litter the beaches at St. Michael. Most of the beached boats were cut up for firewood during and after World War II. (Arthur Peterson)

131

The Tanana *heads up the Yukon for Fort Yukon with a light deck load and a full cargo of petroleum in midsummer 1980. (Arthur Peterson)*

looks funny to have a big, old tree sticking up from your stern," he says. "The *Kantishna* has three props, so she could still limp home on the other two."

Up in the wheelhouse, Captain Keith Horton, a slight, quiet man, deftly moves the brass rudder tillers from side to side, picking out the channels. A brass Seth Thomas chronometer chimes ship's bells on the hour and half hour. The bright orange display on the digital fathometer flickers, 14, 10, 11, 9, 9, 7, feet of water beneath the hull.

The *Tanana* heads straight for the bank. With the fathomether reading barely six feet, Horton shuts off the engines, then shoves one throttle into reverse and one into forward as he swings the tillers hard over. Boat and barges (with a combined length of nearly 300 feet) slide into a narrow channel within spitting distance of the bank.

Up on the bow of the *OB-4* deckhands man-handle long sounding poles, fending off over-hanging "sweepers" and checking inboard depth of the river bottom. Sixteen feet long and painted different colors every foot, the sounding poles are indispensable for testing shallow water at the bow of the barges, some 200 feet forward of the fathometer's sensor.

Uncharted and unmarked, the Tanana and Yukon rivers demand a lot of experience of navigators. To the untrained eye, the river's surface reveals nothing. "You pretty much got to keep it all in your head," Horton remarks. "The water is showing up pretty good today. If there's any wind you have trouble seeing it."

Yutana's captains come up through the ranks. There's no other way. Horton apprenticed his trade with two years as a deckhand, three years as second mate, a year as first mate, and two more as a pilot before he gained his command. He learned at the side of the company's master navigators, Al Brown and Dave Walker. Then, as all skippers must do before they receive their license, Horton was required to draw the entire 1,600-mile navigable length of the Yukon, plus the Tanana, from memory.

Picking Out the Channels

At Twenty-Mile Slough, deckhands lower one of the two pilot boats over the side. Using the fast outboard runabout, Pilot Hnilicka will scout out the best route ahead of the slower moving *Tanana*.

Hnilicka is soon speeding out of sight around the next bend. He'll range ahead for more than

Crew of Tanana *prepares to hoist pilot boat aboard after negotiating Squaw Crossing on the Tanana River. Outboards are equipped with radio, depth finder. (Henry S. Kaiser, Jr.)*

Yutana barges carry tanker trucks loaded with fuel for delivery to remote sites away from the river without pumping facilities. (Arthur Peterson)

12 hours, returning to the *Tanana* only long enough to refuel and grab a bite to eat.

In the wheelhouse, Charlie's voice crackles over the radio, "Wrap right around this point and stick pretty close [to the bank]. We don't want to get very far out here. Then point her right at the island. That's your absolute edge right where you are; you don't want to get out any further than that."

A few miles farther down at Martinez Crossing, the pilot boat comes speeding back, describes a tight 360-degree turn, and races away in an arrow-straight line toward a point on the opposite shore. "That line I just drew there [with the pilot boat's wake] is your upper marker. Use that spruce hanging off the bank down there for the lower marker." Responding to the radio, Horton swings the barges around and aims across the river for the new channel.

"These crossings are the key to the river," Horton explains. "They're constantly changing and you never know from one trip to the next where the channel will be. Charlie and I have to be up all the time on this river [the Tanana]. It gets pretty nervous when the water is bad and you're picking your way for 15 or 16 hours straight.

"In the fall when the air temperature is colder than the water, the fog gets so thick you can't see the bow. That's when we tie up and wait for it to lift."

Steaks and Chocolate Chip Cookies

At midday, the *Tanana* swings around and noses into the bank for the noon meal break. Peaches, pineapple slices, beef stew, biscuits, ham and beans and apple pie ala mode are on the menu. The engines are kept running to counteract the current and the big 57-inch propellers, located right beneath the mess room, set up an awful vibration. Dishes vibrate across the table and the racket is so loud conversation is impossible. Deckhands and engineers wolf lunch and hastily return to work.

Dinner is a repeat of the midday routine with roast chicken, salad, roast potatoes, broccoli with cheese sauce (typical youngsters, the deckhands won't eat vegetables), pie or cake on the table. A quick meal, then return to work.

"Feed the crew well if you expect them to work well," is an ironclad rule in this business. Yutana spares no expense on groceries and hires competent cooks to see they're well prepared.

Though only in her mid-20s, Cook Margaret Garrett is among the best in the business. "Saturday night is always steak night, whether we're on the river or in port," she says. "But the rest of the time I try to add as much variety as I can and seldom serve the same meal twice. We'll be having huevos rancheros, Chinese food, plenty of meat, pies and cakes—whatever the boys like. I traded some salmon for bear meat with the cook of the *Kantishna* when we were in Nenana. Sometimes, on the run to Fort Yukon, some of the crew will take the pilot boat out fishing and come back with salmon or grayling."

Margaret learned her trade on a crab processor and in the oil fields of Texas, a couple of spots where culinary imagination is quite limited. But she makes liberal use of cookbooks, ordering any special ingredients from headquarters in Nenana. The traditional pot of hot coffee is always ready on the sideboard at any hour and there's usually a dish or two of Margaret's fresh brownies, chocolate chip cookies or vanilla wafers.

With the long summer twilight finally fading, the *Tanana* noses into the north bank and ties up for the night, just past 10 p.m. It's been a long day. Seventeen hours of hard work and anxiety.

Though the *Tanana* and other Yutana tugs are equipped with video tape decks and a library of the latest films, nobody is watching tonight.

Aerial view of Tanana *offloading at Galena. Note how tug remains in deep water with barges tied close inshore, unloaded with crane. (Arthur Peterson)*

They'll have a bare six hours to catch a few winks before tackling the river again. The Yukon is not yet in sight and the worst is yet to come.

Aground at Squaw Crossing

At 4:45 a.m. the *Tanana* is underway again. Pilot Hnilicka is out ahead in the runabout; Captain Horton is at the helm. Squaw Crossing, the most notorious on the Tanana, is just ahead.

"These crossings are the worst," states Horton. "The channel often runs clear across the river, from bank to bank. Most are named for some trapper or prospector who lived nearby. Squaw dates from the days when there was an Indian fish camp here. The story is that so many pilots were busy watching the squaws, they went aground.

"It's been so bad out here this summer we've spent hours looking for a channel." To maintain steerage, water must pass over the big four-by-eight-foot rudders faster than the river is flowing. For the *Tanana* this means a downstream speed of nine or ten knots. If she meets a bar, she'll meet it like a battering ram, driving the barges hard aground.

Hnilicka's voice comes over the wheelhouse radio speaker, "The channel keeps moving. It must have moved 30 feet since we last went through here. We're going to have to walk her through sideways."

Nearly a mile across near its mouth, the river is dotted with islands and bars. Stumps, stranded logs and other debris jut from the surface as far as the eye can see and, to the uninitiated, it appears as if one could almost walk across the soupy water without getting his feet wet.

A sudden lurch and the barges are aground.

Horton snaps the throttles in reverse and applies full power. He'll try to back off the bar before the current sets the barges too firmly and before new silt and sand can be deposited beneath the upstream end. With her twin six-cylinder Enterprise diesels racing with their full 1,800 horsepower and props thrashing the water to a gray froth, the *Tanana* strains to free her charges.

No use. The barges won't budge.

Horton now lets the current swing the *Tanana* around, so tug and barges are headed upstream. "We'll try to wash them off with the props," he explains. "Sometimes we have to cast off from the barges and pull alongside, then wash the sand from beneath each side of the barges. Earlier this year we were stuck here for 22 hours. I hope it's not going to be that bad this time."

Alternating throttles and rudders, Horton swings tug and barges in big arcs, trying to work his way free while at the same time throwing prop wash beneath the hull to wash out the sand. Orange numbers flick over the fathometer—3, 8,

Aerial view of harbor at St. Michael. Black Navigation facilities are at lower end of cove, tank farm at upper right. Entire shoreline of cove was once covered with steamboats.   (Arthur Peterson)

Yutana barges carry forklift trucks that can quickly offload deck cargo over timber camps laid from barge to shore. (Bob Bune)

4, 2. Fifty yards out, the pilot boat races around the tug like some frenzied water bug. Hnilicka's scouting for deeper water, calling out soundings over the radio as he goes.

Just as suddenly as they grounded, the barges are free and the riverbanks begin to slide by once more.

Al Brown is fond of saying, "It's not whether you run aground that counts. Everybody does that. It's what you do after you hit that matters."

But trouble seems to come in bunches.

Within minutes the radio announces, "I've blown the engine on the boat [pilot boat]." The runabout is retrieved, hoisted onto the fantail and the *Tanana* heaves to until repairs can be made.

Because they're far from any emergency help and can only contact Nenana by radio (which frequently doesn't work because of atmospheric conditions), Yutana's crews are on their own. Each tug is equipped to make its own running

repairs. The skills of engineers and deck crew are the only things they can depend on in a crisis. For repairs to propellers and rudders, the *Tanana* is equipped with bow tanks that can be flooded to raise the stern out of the water.

Underway again with the Yukon nearly in sight. The only clear channel seems to be a narrow lead, less than 100 feet wide, between a large sandbar and a small treeless island. Horton eases down into it at dead slow speed, intending to "thread the needle" with no room to spare.

Hnilicka radios, "This channel dead ends down here at the tip of the island. That upper bar is steadily moving down this way. It wasn't near so bad when I first went through here. You're going to have to put the barges down into this hole, then back through the gap in the bar."

He's describing a small gap in the bar that is now outboard of the *Tanana*. The maneuver will describe a rough "T" with the boat and barges moving down the channel that forms the top, then reversing and backing through the hole that forms the leg.

Horton will earn his pay on this one.

Sliding down along the island at a slow walk, he stops the barges at the point where the pilot boat is perched above the end of the lead. In the meantime, Hnilicka has dropped two bright orange plastic buoys to mark the limits of the gap in the bar. Horton then reverses the engines, gives her hard starboard rudder and squeaks through the pass.

His only comment, "Try that one with the current pushing down against you."

On the Yukon

At 10 a.m. the *Tanana* swings into the Yukon and is tied up at the village of Tanana by 10:30. Deckhands haul large steel cables ashore, wading through yapping Indian dogs, to tie tug and barges to the bank. There are no mooring facilities on the Yukon; unloading is directly onto the riverbank. Timbers are run out from the barges to the beach, and the forklifts that are carried aboard quickly move freight ashore.

There's little conversation. Everyone seems to know his job and mate and deckhands go through an unloading routine they've handled dozens of times before. "By this time of the season, the deck crew has things working pretty well," explains Captain Horton. "It's a lot easier if we get some experienced deckhands back each year. The first couple of trips with a green crew are pretty ragged."

Wayne Pattee, who got his start on the Mississippi and Ohio river boats, returns to his home in Arkansas every winter. Keith Horton has a home in Michigan. Eunice Lilly is spending her eleventh summer on the river. When the season ends, she'll visit relatives in Anchorage, then go on to Wisconsin. Deckhand Mark Boehm, a native of Southern California, started on the boats last year and spent the winter running a trap line in the Alaska interior. "I always wanted to spend the winter in a log cabin in the woods," he says, "and last year I did it."

Offloading at Tanana is completed by 9 p.m. and the diesel fuel from *Stewart* has been pumped into *OB-4*. The empty *Stewart* will be left tied up to the bank just above the village to be picked up on the return trip.

Now in the deep water of the Yukon, the *Tanana* has clear sailing downstream, following the bends in the river at ten knots. The crew now stands regular six-hour watches. About midnight the *Rampart* passes heading upstream to Nenana from a trip to Galena.

At 10:15 the following morning [day three] the tug and her single barge ease into the bank at Campion to offload fuel on the *OB-4*. The Campion radar site, perched atop a hill, is connected by pipeline to terminal fittings on the riverbank. Archie Thurmond, Yutana's agent, has brought his truck-mounted pumping rig over the dirt road from Galena to force the diesel fuel up the pipeline to Campion. Deckhands, fighting off clouds of mosquitoes, haul the big hoses over the side, connect them to the pump and settle down to ten uneventful hours of pumping.

Campion delivery completed, the *Tanana* drops down six miles to Galena. Here, Thurmond's crews work all night with the aid of powerful floodlights mounted on the *Tanana's* wheelhouse, to unload deck cargo by crane.

By 8 a.m. lines are cast off and the *Tanana* moves out into the Yukon heading home for another load. After the downstream trip, the voyage back to Nenana with empty barges will be a piece of cake.

XI

A YUKON RIVERBOAT ALBUM

A Yukon Riverboat Album

The Yutana Fleet

(Bob Bune)

TANANA

Length: 110 feet   Beam: 35 feet   Draft: 44 inches
Net tonnage: 228   Gross Tonnage: 450   Screws: 2   Rudders: 8
Power: 2 Enterprise DMG-6 diesels, generating 600 horsepower each.
Electricity: 2 diesel generators producing 75 kw.
Fuel capacity: 13,000 gallons   Fresh Water Capacity: produced on board.
Berths: 18   Crew: 12   Built: 1953, Albina Shipyard, Portland, Oregon

INDEPENDENCE

Length: 74 feet   Beam: 24 feet   Draft: 32 inches

Net tonnage: 86   Gross tonnage: 185   Screws: 3   Rudders: 3

Power: 3 8-V-71-T GMC diesels generating 350 horsepower each.

Electricity: 4-71 GMC diesel generator producing 50 kw.

Fuel Capacity: 4,500 gallons   Fresh Water Capacity: 1,200 gallons

Crew: 6   Built: former LCM acquired from Roland Moody in 1974. Formerly twin screw. Completely rebuilt 1982 with additional 8 feet of length and 8 feet of width.

RAMPART

Length: 90 feet   Beam: 28 feet   Draft: 30 inches
Net tonnage: 108   Gross tonnage: 225   Screws: 3   Rudders: 6
Power: 3 8V-71-T GMC diesels generating 350 horsepower each.
Electricity: 4-71 GMC diesel generator producing 50 kw.
Fuel Capacity: 6,000 gallons   Fresh Water Capacity: 2,500 gallons
Crew: 8   Built: 1965 by Albina Shipyard, Portland, Oregon for Weaver Brothers. Acquired by
Yutana 1968. Completely rebuilt 1982.

HUSKY

Length: 70 feet	Beam: 26 feet	Draft: 29 inches
Net tonnage: 86	Gross tonnage: 150	Screws: 4 Rudders: 4

Power: 4 671 GMC diesels generating 250 horsepoewr each.
Electricity: 4-71 GMC diesel generator producing 50 kw.
Fuel Capacity: 3,500 gallons   Fresh Water Capacity: 1,500 gallons
Crew: 4   Built: Former LCM of Sumested Navigation acquired by Yutana in 1975. Rebuilt 1982.

PAT

Length: 67 feet   Beam: 30 feet   Draft: 29 inches
Net tonnage: 102   Gross tonnage: 215   Screws: 2   Rudders: 4
Power: 4 671 GMC diesels generating 250 horsepower each.
Electricity: 4-71 GMC diesel generator producing 50 kw.
Fuel Capacity: 3,500 gallons   Fresh Water Capacity: 1,500 gallons
Crew: 10   Built: Former LCM acquired from Harlan Eggleston 1975. Completely rebuilt by welding two LCMs together in 1981.

KANTISHNA

Length: 71 feet   Beam: 23 feet   Draft: 48 inches
Net tonnage: 92   Gross tonnage: 181   Screws: 3   Rudders: 3
Power: 3 8-V-71-T GMC diesels generating 350 horsepower each.
Electricity: 4-71 GMC diesel generator producing 50 kw.
Fuel Capacity: 3,000 gallons   Fresh Water Capacity: 1,500 gallons
Crew: 8   Built: Acquired from Weaver Brothers in 1968; formerly named Emma II—
widened 8 feet and lengthened 10 feet at Nenana in 1980.

Alaska Railroad's General J. W. Jacobs *departs Nenana in 1920s for voyage up the Yukon to Eagle. Note absence of barges or deck cargo. (Anchorage Historical and Fine Arts Museum)*

BIBLIOGRAPHY

Cohen, Stan, *The Forgotten War,* Pictoral Histories Publishing Co., 1981
Cohen, Stan, *The Streets Were Paved With Gold,* Pictoral Histories Publishing Co., 1977
Cohen, Stan, *Yukon River Steamboats,* Pictoral Histories Publishing Co., 1982
Downs, Art, *Paddlewheels on the Frontier,* Superior Publishing Co., 1972
Fejes, Claire, *Villagers,* Random House, 1981
Kitchener, L. D., *Flag Over the North,* Superior Publishing Co., 1954
Knutson, Arthur E., *Sternwheels on the Yukon,* Snohomish Publishing Co., 1979
Mathews, Richard, *The Yukon,* Holt, Rinehart and Winston, 1968
McCurdy, H. W., *Marine History of the Pacific Northwest,* Superior Publishing Co., 1966
Naske, Claus M. and Slotnick, Herman E., *Alaska–A History of the 49th State,* William B. Eerdmans Publishing Co., 1979
Satterfield, Archie, *After the Gold Rush,* J. P. Lippincott Co., 1976
Satterfield, Archie, *Chilcoot Pass,* Alaska Northwest Publishing Co., 1973
Satterfield, Archie, *Exploring the Yukon River,* The Mountaineers, 1975
Stumer, Harold Merritt, *This Was Klondike Fever,* Superior Publishing Co., 1978
Wilson, William H., *Railroad in the Clouds,* Pruett Publishing Co., 1977

Other Publications, various issues

Alaska Construction and Oil
Alaska Fest
Alaska Geographic
Alaska Journal
Alaska Magazine
Alaska Weekly
Cariboo and Northwest Digest
Columbia Sentinel
Fairbanks News Miner
Master, Mate and Pilot
Pacific Historical Review

Other Sources

Alaska Railroad, Anchorage
Alaska State Museum Archives, Juneau
Anchorage Historical and Fine Arts Museum
MacBride Museum, Whitehorse
National Archives and Records Service, Military Field Branch, Suitland, Maryland
National Archives and Records Service, Navy and Old Army, Washington, D.C.
National Archives and Records Service, Seattle
Seattle Public Library
University of Alaska Archives, Fairbanks
University of Washington, Pacific Northwest Collection, Seattle
U.S. Coast Guard, Anchorage
U.S. Custom House records (various)
Yukon Archives, Whitehorse

British Yukon Navigation Co.'s Casca *and* White Horse *docked at the Whitehorse waterfront in 1920. White Pass & Yukon Railroad transfers cargo directly at dockside. (Yukon Archives)*

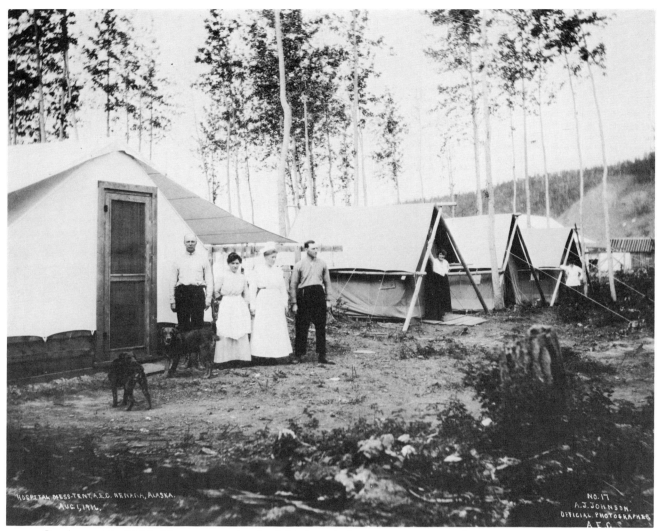

On August 1, 1916, Nenana consisted of this hospital tent, mess tents and construction crew tents, a base camp for the building of the Alaska Railroad. (Anchorage Historical and Fine Arts Museum)

INDEX

Sod-roofed cabin festooned with hunter's trophy moose antlers is typical of Native residences remote from Yukon villages. (Bob Bune)

PHOTO INDEX

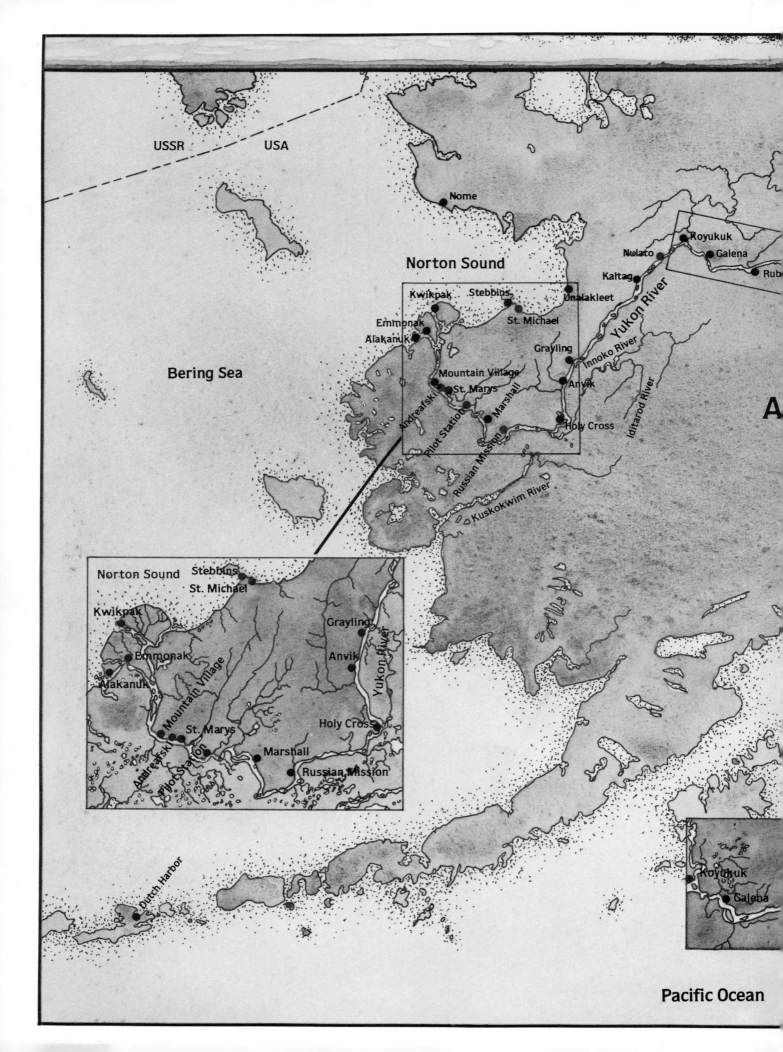